S0-AZQ-323

# BIG SAM

Sam Churchill

# BIG
# SAM

1965

DOUBLEDAY & COMPANY, INC., GARDEN CITY, NEW YORK

Library of Congress Catalog Card Number 65-13975
Copyright © 1965 by Sam Churchill
All Rights Reserved
Printed in the United States of America

To the Man and Woman

Who Lived These Events,

My Parents

Samuel J. Churchill

Caroline Snow Churchill

# CONTENTS

*Chapter 1*

## IN THE BEGINNING

It used to be the main line of a logging railroad but now the ties and steel rails are gone and bulldozers have leveled the old right of way into a convenient access road. You can follow the road for miles and miles, deep into the moody silence of the Oregon Coast Range mountains, and never lose sight of the trampled, bareheaded hills that once were covered with forest.

This is the way you'll find the land if you turn onto this unmarked forest road twenty miles southeast of the Columbia River town of Astoria in Clatsop County, Oregon.

This is logger land. This is the land my father, Big Sam Churchill, loved. This is the land where I was born and lived my boyhood. It was here, in my growing years, that teams of sweating, straining men and monstrous sled-mounted machines ranged in pursuit of the seemingly endless stands of centuries-old Douglas fir, hemlock, spruce, and cedar.

This was a land whose wealth of trees was beyond the wildest expectations of turn-of-the-century loggers. It was a land whose vigor and beauty would never end. As the big machines with their human masters slashed their way to daylight at the crest of one ridge there seemed to be always more tree-loaded ridges, canyons, and peaks beyond.

It was of this land that my Uncle Marshall Churchill wrote so fondly to his brother Sam in Maine in 1902. "We leave more saw logs to rot than they grow in the whole damn state of Maine," he boasted.

When the letter arrived the man who was to become my

father took it over to a lighted lantern hanging from a length
of wire hooked to an overhead rafter. Outside the Maine
logging camp bunkhouse that housed him and two dozen
others the winter woods were white and frozen. The bitter
cold drilled under the bark of spruce and pine, froze the sap,
and set up such internal stresses that trunks would burst.

Big Sam straddled a rickety bunkhouse bench and spread
the letter out flat in front of him. He read slowly and carefully. His lips sounded out each word because as a boy it
was often necessary that he spend more time working in
his father's potato fields than in school. At the end of the
third grade his formal education ended. It wasn't a decision
of choice. It was one forced by the workings of the potato
market and farmer economics. The farm was poor and the
crops never seemed to return enough to pay for the luxury
of hired help.

Finishing the letter, Big Sam took it over and handed
it to the camp boss. "Tomorrow or maybe the next day
I guess I'll be going West," he said.

The boss looked up with a frown. He was engrossed in
a poker game where pinches of snoose and chewing tobacco
served as stakes. In the winter camps payday usually came
in the spring. Since there was little or no cash in a camp
until payday card-game stakes had to be improvised.

It wasn't Big Sam's interruption of the poker game that
brought the frown to the boss's face. It was his declared intention of quitting. The boss would rather lose any half-
dozen men from his crew than lose Big Sam. He motioned
to a quieter corner of the smelly, stale-aired, barnlike room.
In the dim glow of another lantern he read the letter.

"Marsh is crazy as hell," he said, handing the letter back.
"I know. I been out there. That country is a man-killer.
If you ain't climbing up, you're climbing down. They's
hardly a level place big enough to set your ass. When it ain't
raining it's blowing and most of the year it's doing both."

"I can get along with the wind and rain," said Big Sam with a shrug. "It's better than this snow and cold."

As the train moved across the upper reaches of the Midwest and on into North Dakota and eastern Montana there were moments of misgiving when the sameness of the land began to bother Big Sam. He kept watching for the monstrous trees and rugged, exciting land that his brother Marshall had kept writing about. By the time the train reached Livingston, Montana, Big Sam was tired of waiting and ready to turn back. He pushed the remainder of his ticket under the wicket of a ticket window and voiced his disillusionment and intention of returning to Maine.

The ticket clerk urged him to go on. "You're just getting into the real West," he argued. "God's country is the next thousand miles straight ahead."

Back on the train and with the click of wheels on rail joints counting off the miles west he felt suddenly relaxed, at ease and grateful to the ticket man who had urged him to continue westward.

With the train grunting at a snail's pace up the eastern rise of the Rocky Mountains, and standing on the rear platform of the observation car with track dirt and cinders swirling around him, Big Sam studied the massive contours of land and escarpments jutting skyward from the roots of the earth. There was something wildly exhilarating in the scene, in knowing that he was becoming a part of this magnificent land where mountain peaks seemed to hold up the sky and creeks were the size of eastern rivers.

He thought dreamily of what lay ahead. Although there was no clue, other than Marshall's letters, that his imagination could build an image on, he had already seen enough to know that whatever lay ahead for him in this raw tangle of mountains, timber, and rivers would be to his liking.

He turned, and looking back along the lengthening distance of track falling away behind the rear of the train, said good-by to his home state of Maine forever.

It was mid-December 1902 when Big Sam Churchill arrived in Portland, Oregon. There were still patches of virgin timber in what are now residential areas of the city. Standing in the doorway of the Pullman car, he looked out over the heads of the hurrying throngs that crowded the covered platforms of the Union Station. There was a hurry and excitement here, a vigor and independence that no longer exerted itself in the East. It seeped into a man's system, swirled him along like a chip in an ocean current. This was a land of muscle, bull teams, and timber. It was a land that would spawn baronial empires of wealth, prestige, and power. For a man the age of Big Sam, thirty-two, the opportunities were unlimited. For a man with a little cash, success could be almost immediate. And Big Sam did have cash—almost five thousand dollars nestled safely against the iron-hard frame of his body in a crude but sturdy hand-sewn canvas money belt. It was money he had saved from the hard-earned pittance paid by operators of Maine lumber camps. It was money that invested at the right time and in the right place could reap him a fortune.

But Big Sam didn't come West to put together a fortune; or to build an empire that would perpetuate his name. Not that he was unsympathetic with such goals. He admired men like Simon Benson, Simcoe and Fred Chapman, the Weyerhaeusers, and dozens of others including his own uncle, Abraham Crouse. They already were or soon would be names to reckon with in the world of ax and saw, skid roads, and the warning cry of "Timberrrrrr" as the rooted giants came crashing down to the virgin earth.

Those early days spawned many a timber baron but a big share of them started out with little more than guts, a bull team to drag their logs to water, and more guts.

There was wealth in those green hills of timber for as James

J. Hill, the railroad magnate and financier, once said: "One acre of timberland contains more traffic tonnage for a railroad than do fifty acres of wheatland."

At thirty-two years of age Big Sam came West as a toiler. He was admirably suited for such a role. His lean hundred and ninety-five pounds was packed flat against an iron-hard belly and a length of frame that was a hair over six feet. His shoulders filled the doorway of the Pullman car, frame to frame. His face was set square and rested on a blocklike chin and heavy jaw line that bespoke a man capable of great physical effort, stubbornness, and a will to work. The eyes were friendly, trusting, and weather-bleached blue.

As he reached for a handrail to swing from the car a porter noticed the size of the hand and fingers and smiled in a mixture of satisfaction and awe. "Welcome to Oregon, suh," he said, "we need men like you." Always a modest man, Big Sam nodded in embarrassment at the obvious compliment and hoped none of the others crowded around had heard.

As he was about to step down to the little platform stand below the bottom step of the car a voice called out from far back in the throng. "Sam! Sam! Over here." Although he hadn't heard that voice for several years there was no mistaking it. He looked in the direction of the sound and a pleased smile etched crow's-feet at the corners of his eyes as he spotted a familiar face.

"Marsh," he called with a grin. The two men moved toward each other, shouldering their way through openings in the crowd as easily as switch engines in the adjoining freight yards were nudging their way among the hundreds of cars.

Coming within reach of each other, the brothers locked hands in a grip that might have cracked bones in fingers of lesser size and strength. There was no mistaking these two men for anything but brothers. But under the surface there were great differences. Marshall, the younger by eight years, was volatile, enthusiastic, and often totally unpredictable. Big Sam, ninth in a family of thirteen, was quiet, almost shy, and unmindful of the tremendous inborn potentials for leadership he possessed. And so it was that whenever the two were together it was Marshall, the younger, who took the lead and made the decisions.

As the two men left the station Marshall led the way toward a livery rig he had rented. "There's something I want you to see," he explained. His voice was high with excitement and his eyes glinted with anticipation and pleasure.

"You're married," said Big Sam. "You got a wife."

The voiced suspicions of his older brother sent the younger one into a fit of laughter. "You talk like Pa," he chided. "Neither one of you think I got a lick of sense." He stopped laughing and his voice and eyes became serious. "I don't want a woman, leastways a steady woman, yet," he said, taking one of Big Sam's two heavily laden suitcases—his only luggage— and falling in step. "There's too much to do, too much to see out here. This is big country. A man's gotta be free to roam."

Reaching the livery rig, they tossed Big Sam's suitcases in the back behind the seat and drove to a high piece of ground on the downtown fringe of the city. Reaching the crest, Marshall faced the horse north and a little west to where he judged the Willamette and the Columbia rivers met. It was one of those unexpected sparkling December days that so often blooms over the rainy coastal regions of Oregon. The clouds and hovering mists had gone into hiding and left the sun, brilliant and alone, in a rain-washed sky. Marshall motioned in the direction of the unseen Pacific Ocean. "This is what I've been writing about," he said.

Big Sam leaned forward from the buggy seat. Ahead of him and on both sides and to the rear was mountain after mountain of forest, stacked one behind the other like pieces of scenery, stored upright, on a stage.

"Trees, Sam," said Marshall, feeling for the round metal step on the side of the buggy, and locating it, stepping to the ground. "They's probably two hundred logging outfits, big and little, working out there with horses, bull teams, and steam donkey engines," he said, "and they ain't cut a hole big enough to see."

He paused to admire again the sight with his own eyes and let what he had just said soak solidly into the mind of his brother. He sucked in a lung full of crisp, clear December air and seemed to hold it a moment with a look of pleasure and relish such as another might savor a sip of quality brandy. As he released the air it sped away in a whisp of vapor toward the west.

"They'll be logging here a thousand years from now," he predicted. "You mark what I say, Sam. A thousand years from now."

Big Sam sat as though rooted to the buggy seat. He had seen the vast, flowing pineries of the Lake States which fire and ax had already turned into a wasteland of stumps. Great numbers of the big mills had already gathered their crews and established beachheads in fresh stands of pine in the South. He had done his share of cutting in the familiar forested areas of his home state Maine and in New Hampshire, Vermont, and across the border in Canada's New Brunswick and parts of Quebec. But never, even in his wildest dreams, had he imagined anything like this.

Confronted with it at last, he just sat and in a voice that was little more than an awed whisper kept saying over and over as though talking to himself: "It's big. God A'mighty, Marsh, it's big."

It was one of the few times in his life when he would take the name of the Lord in vain.

An old Maine logger, an uncle of Big Sam and Marshall, had a logging operation some twenty miles north of Portland near the town of St. Helens and several miles up a small stream, named Milton Creek, from the Columbia River. His name was Abraham Crouse. He came out from Maine in 1891 to prove to himself that no matter what some folks were saying there were no trees in the world with the possible exception of California redwoods that grew to ten feet in diameter and from two to three hundred feet tall.

He wrote back to Maine after his arrival and admitted that: "I know damn well it's a lie, but I've seen them."

It was a time when Douglas fir, named after David Douglas, distinguished botanist and early scientific visitor to old Fort Vancouver on the banks of the Columbia River at what is now Vancouver, Washington, could be had for prices ranging from virtually nothing to $40 or $60 an acre. Some tracts included water sites where a man could fall or roll the trees directly into the water and float them to the mill.

Uncle Abe, as Dad and Uncle Marshall called him, lost all interest in the thicket-like spruce and pine of the Northeast. He was anxious to tackle a tree that shook the ground and rattled the heavens when it keeled over from its stump.

In 1892 he moved his family West and started a small logging operation on Milton Creek. He was looking for husky, young men who loved the feel and smell of their own sweat. He found two to his liking in Big Sam and Marshall Churchill, sons of his sister Ann, a gentle, hard-working woman who had married a Washburn, Maine, potato farmer, Job Churchill.

By the time Big Sam joined his Uncle Abe's crew the doughty old logger had gotten rid of his bull teams and was dragging logs from cutting areas to the banks of Milton Creek with a steam-powered donkey engine. A wooden barrier, called a splash dam, was built across the creek upstream from the cutting area. At intervals, but mostly in the spring of the year when rains and melting snows raised the water level, the gates of the dam were closed. Water trapped behind the barrier would quickly rise into a storage pool. When there were sufficient logs scattered along the downstream banks the gates would be opened and the wall of water sweeping free of the dam would sluice the logs the several miles to the Columbia River. Once gathered into rafts in nearby lagoons the logs were towed by tugboats to sawmills along the river.

The drives were cruel, dangerous, physical effort that left Big Sam and the others soaked, cold, and exhausted at the end of the normal twelve-hour working day. The only thing that made it bearable was that Uncle Abe worked chest-deep in the icy water right along with the rest of his crew.

Finishing his logging operation on Milton Creek, Uncle Abe bought more timber downstream several miles on a creek known as Tide Creek. The creek spilled into a tidal section of the river near a mist-coated, waterlogged piece of land that Lewis and Clark had named Deer Island. The two explorers had camped there on their way down the Columbia River on November 5, 1805, and again on the return trip east on March 28, 1806.

Clark reported in his journal that the party's hunters killed seven deer on the island. Three years after his arrival in Portland, Big Sam felt himself almost a pioneer, but the glow of his pioneer spirit was never able to spark into a flame as long as he knew that there had been white men hunting and gazing upon these same trees, and possibly drinking water out of this same creek sixty-five years before he was born.

## Chapter 2

## THE FIRST COMERS

By the time Big Sam arrived in Oregon in 1902 white men had long been hacking at the forest giants that stood like hair on a dog's back from the crest of the Cascades west to the wet sands of the Pacific.

Early traders and explorers investigating the coastal waters were among the first to fell some of these magnificent spires that grew straight as a ship's mast and so tall that their tops were often hidden from view by low hanging mists.

In the heavy rainfall regions of the Coast Range mountains, heavily populated with hemlock and Douglas fir, Nature packed them so closely on an acre of land that the green arms of their tops interlaced. Here were millions of acres of tree-cloaked wealth where the sun's direct rays never reached the ground. Moisture, humus, and forest waste of a thousand years lay molding, rotting, and settling in a constant cycle of life and death and reabsorption into the giver of life, the ground.

Shipmasters often sent scouting crews ashore in search of perfect specimens for replacement of worn or broken spars, hull planks and decking.

The Lewis and Clark party hacked out a fifty by fifty foot clearing on the south shore of the Columbia River near its mouth and erected a stockade and shelter in which they spent the winter of 1805–6. They named it Fort Clatsop. The spot is now a national monument and a replica of the old fort replaces the original that Nature long ago reclaimed.

It was from these same forests that the first units of what

is now Astoria, Oregon, were built. Employees of the Pacific Fur Company, a trading firm organized by John Jacob Astor and his associates to tap the wealth of fur in the region, felled and shaped dozens of the giants into timbers for construction of Fort Astoria in 1811. By strange coincidence it was to this place, the town of Astoria, that Big Sam brought his bride one hundred years, almost to the day, later. And it was here, in this historic town now grown to a bustling community supported out over the Columbia River tide flats on piling, that I was born. A half-dozen sawmills screamed their way through a half million feet of Clatsop County timber a day. The old fort, its disintegrated remains buried under brush and rubbish in a vacant lot, lay hidden, undisturbed, and forgotten in the frantic rush of this new era.

Upriver and on the opposite bank in what is now Washington State, Dr. John McLoughlin, head of the Hudson's Bay Company's Columbia River department with headquarters at Fort Vancouver, had in 1827 built a small water-powered sawmill to supply the fort's building needs. It was also his thought that there was a potential for lumber as a valuable trade commodity. In 1828–29 he tested his theory by shipping some of the mill's surplus to the Sandwich (Hawaiian) Islands where it sold for a handsome $100 a thousand board feet.

Twenty years later, in 1849, there were thirty mills in Oregon hungrily working to supply the needs of California gold seekers at prices ranging from $80 to $100 a thousand. A number of those mills were in the Astoria area.

Cyrus Reed and Stephan Coffin started a steam mill at the foot of Jefferson Street in Portland, Oregon, in 1850. Many of the more pessimistic of the village's uneasy population freely predicted that the damn thing was bound to blow up and when it did it would take the town of Portland with it.

Lumber demands in the California gold fields were tapering off and market outlets in other areas tightened. But the region's early sawmill and logging operators found a new outlet for their wares closer to home. Settlers by the thousands came overland by horse, mule team and afoot, or around Cape Horn by boat. They needed lumber for homes, barns, corn cribs, and wagons. Ships and docks at which those ships could load and unload supplies had to be built.

Instead of declining, the region's infant lumber industry rolled up its sleeves and went to work supplying this new market. Henry Yesler built a mill in Seattle. The old skid road over which he dragged his logs by bull team is now a street, Yesler Way. Colonel Michael T. Simmons started a mill near Olympia as early as 1845. A gold strike in southern Oregon sent the lumber market in that area soaring to $250 a thousand by 1852.

By 1869 most every Oregon community could boast at least one mill, large or small, either in or near it. Men and machines were turning out seventy-five million board feet a year and settlers and gold seekers were howling for more. By 1909 the Polson Logging Company on Washington State's Olympic Peninsula was cutting almost double that figure each year by itself, and the annual cut in Oregon was at the two billion foot mark with a record peak in 1952 of a hair under nine billion board feet, enough in terms of houses to build almost a million average homes.

In 1909 a quality Douglas fir log measuring ninety-two to one hundred feet in length and with a top diameter of twenty-seven to twenty-eight inches was worth from $22 to $28 in the water. And Nature loved her Douglas fir. She packed them a thousand strong to the acre and as though to assure Man an inexhaustible supply, she marched them across valley, hogback, and coastal plain from the top of the Cascades to the Pacific and from British Columbia to California.

But as she had so often done in the past, Nature underestimated the capabilities of this creature, Man, she had spawned. She didn't anticipate the coming of such men as California's John Dolbeer who developed the steam-powered donkey engine that was to virtually replace animal power in the woods by the turn of the century.

She failed to weigh the effects on her forestry program of such men as the bearded Michigan logger, Ephraim Shay, who did for the transportation phase of logging what Dolbeer had done for the short haul, by developing his powerful, fearless geared engine, the Shay. With the aid of the Shay and other special types of locomotives such as the Heisler and Climax, the distance of a stand of timber from water was no longer a problem for the logger. He laid wooden or steel rails from tidewater to hogback, to ridge, to mountain peak, across river valley and tree-choked canyon, and the Shay followed with empty cars to be loaded. And when they were loaded it hauled them to the mill.

Where the rails couldn't go he stretched steel cables from the tops of trees and lifted the logs free of the ground, or lifted one end high to clear obstacles such as stumps and snags. With these devices, which he called skylines (aerial tramways), he bridged canyons and reached the almost inaccessible heights too costly to tap with a railroad. In this way Man broke open the fortresses of terrain which Nature had built up over tens of thousands of years to guard and protect this living, shimmering crop of green which was to have been her gift to Man to utilize bit by bit as he found need. She planned it as a self-renewing gift that would go on and on for centuries and centuries of time until Man had firmly established his seed on this earth.

She didn't realize the stamina and determination she had built into such men as the Popes, the Talbots, old Captain Simpson, A. S. Kerry, Johnnie Yeon, the Polsons, the Schafers, and my own father, Big Sam. It was a long hard trip from Maine to Oregon even in 1902. Once a man with the smell of green timber in his blood caught sight of this endless expanse of green-cloaked land there was no holding him back. It made no difference whether he was a baron with thousands of acres of this rich, virgin land to his credit, or a worker whose only material possessions were a can of snoose and the work clothes on his back; the urge was over-powering. He was driven to grab up ax and saw and swing to the attack.

In the decade and a half he had been in the West, Uncle Abraham Crouse had witnessed a number of the profound changes that were taking place. He had seen most of the bull and horse teams pass from the picture. He had watched, and helped shove, the forest line a rather disturbing distance back from the Columbia River and other major waterways. It was disturbing in the sense that it had happened much sooner than he and most of the other early comers to the region had expected. He had noted with satisfaction that tramways and railroads were satisfactorily bridging the dis-tance so that aided by the rails and the faster, more powerful steam donkey engines more timber was reaching tidewater dumps and mills than was dreamed of a few years back when bull teams and skid roads were the link between cutting areas and the water.

He was thinking of these transformations and others that must surely be on the way while on an inspection tour of a new stand of timber he had just gotten hold of. It was a Sunday afternoon and Big Sam was with him. The month was August and the year 1905.

"If you plan on getting yourself some timber you better be getting at it," he suggested to Big Sam. "It's costing more every year and available stands are getting scarce."

"I ain't buying any," replied Big Sam. "Marsh, now, could own timber and make out running his own camp. Me, I come out here to work for wages."

"Marsh is too quick tempered and too foolish with his money," grunted Uncle Abe. "He'd rather spend his free ·ime raisin' hell."

Big Sam was silent for a time. When he spoke again his words were slow and hesitant as though he were still trying to get them properly arranged in his mind.

"Sometimes I think maybe Marsh shouldn't be out here. There's too much freedom for a young fellow to settle down. This country ain't yet solid and set like it is in Maine."

"You need more push, Sam," said Uncle Abe. "You're gettin' old ahead of your years. A little of Marsh's hell raisin' would maybe do you good. He'll try anything once."

Although he spoke the words in half disgust there was a touch of admiration and envy in Uncle Abe's tone. Big Sam caught it and it left him with a sudden feeling of loneliness and inadequacy. He was content to be just Big Sam. But there were times when he wished he were a little more like Marsh.

In the past it had been moments of depression such as he was now experiencing that had sent him to his sister Minnie. Minna was her given name but everyone called her Minnie. There was a little over a year's difference in their ages, which was about as close as you could be chronologically to each other in a family of thirteen children. Minnie had the knack of listening, nodding, and comforting. He judged it was getting on time for a vacation trip to Boston and a visit with Minnie and her husband Stedman Crouse. Analyzing himself on the hike back from the inspection trip to his Uncle Abe's new logging show, Big Sam reached two pairs of overdue conclusions:

(1.) He had been out West three years and was homesick for a sight of the East and the sights and smells of the Maine countryside in the fall with visits to Washburn, Presque Isle, Crouseville, Caribou, and Portland; he was now thirty-five years of age and tired of beans and sow belly on a tin plate in a logging camp cookhouse.

(2.) He was tired of sleeping on straw for a mattress and breathing the thick, heavy stink of unwashed bodies and rain-soaked socks, underwear, and work clothes hung up to dry in tight-shut bunkhouses; logging was his life but there wasn't a Douglas fir tree on earth with the beauty and grace of a good woman. Marsh could go on raising hell and Uncle

Abe could buy every tree between the Cascades and the sea. It put him in near panic to think about it, but Big Sam knew there was no escape. What he had to do was find himself a wife.

The decision to marry and establish his own home, although it frightened him, came so naturally and effortlessly he wondered why he hadn't thought of it before. But finding a girl to match his dreams was not unlike trying to eye-pick the queen tree in a forest. They all looked first-rate at a distance but close up a careful eye could pick out flaws. Though he was eager, Big Sam was careful.

It wasn't until 1908 and in Boston, that he saw what he wanted. And it was his sister Minnie who handled the arrangements. "Now hold on a minute," he pouted, more in panic than anger, when his sister announced she had invited a young woman to dinner, "I'll do my own pickin' and courtin'."

"And end up a bachelor," his sister predicted.

"They's worse things can happen to a man," Big Sam argued.

"And better things," said Minnie, putting her husband in charge of Big Sam while she answered a timid, almost unnoticed knock on the apartment door.

## Chapter 3

## BRIDE FROM BOSTON

Her eyes were blue as an Oregon sky in summer. In East Boston's Stitch and Talk Club, of which she was a member, she was known as "the laughing one." The lines of her neck were soft and full and blended into a dimpled chin and an oval face. On tiptoes she barely reached Big Sam's shoulder. Her name was Caroline M. Snow. She lived in a walk-up apartment with her mother at 200 Princeton Street. She was born and lived in and loved the historic town of cobblestone streets and an unbending aristocracy that was Boston.

It was spring and the year 1910 and Big Sam knew that back home out in Oregon the trilliums and the Oregon grape were in bloom. The yellow faces of tiny Johnny-jump-ups would be looking up at a man from the ground. The alder would be leafing out and clover-like sour grass would be taking up squatters' rights along the banks of mountain streams.

It was spring, that time of year when nature unleashes overpowering drives and urges with the sole purpose of propagating life and perpetuating her clan. Big Sam was having a terrible time. He was sufficiently rational to diagnose his ailment but too shy to prescribe a treatment. His sister Minnie sipped a last cup of breakfast coffee and wondered why physically powerful men like her brother Sam so often seemed to sink into a complete state of shock over so simple and natural a thing as falling in love.

"How do I ask a woman like Caroline Snow to marry me?" he was asking Minnie, for what she was certain was the ten-thousandth time.

"You just ask her."

"How did Stedman ask you?"

"We were riding the elevated and he leaned over and said if I'd marry him it would save him the expense of hiring another clerk because we could both then work in the store."

"You're making fun of me."

"Of course I'm making fun of you," replied Minnie with waning patience. "You're in love with a strong-willed, able-bodied girl who is as smart as a buggy whip. She'll go to Oregon with you, she'll live in a logging camp with you, and she'll make you a good wife. Why do you fret?"

"But what if she says no?"

"Then you start out fresh and look for another."

"You ain't as much comfort as you used to be," sighed Big Sam.

"Of course I'm not," admitted Minnie. "I'm married now and have my own husband to worry about and look after. And besides, he wasn't joking, I work half days in the store and I'm tired."

Long years later, sitting in our logging camp home with winter rains hammering the tar paper roof as we snuggled close to the warmth of our wood burning stove, I recall Dad and Mother reliving the Dad–Minnie conversation and laughing until tears rolled down their cheeks.

On the day following his talk with Minnie, Big Sam bought a diamond engagement ring that out in Oregon would have made the down payment on a quarter section of prime Douglas fir timber.

He first showed it to his sister for her approval. It was she who had contrived to bring Big Sam and Caroline together. Once that had been accomplished she gave full credit to the Lord, saying that it was His will that her best friend and her favorite brother should marry. It hadn't, actually, taken too much maneuvering since the Snow family lived in

a corner apartment over the grocery store operated by
Minnie and her husband.

One glance at the size of the diamond Big Sam had purchased set his sister's eyes to bubbling. "With a ring like that
you should have a harem," she said with a happy grin.

That night Big Sam asked Caroline to marry him. He
waited until the last possible moment, as he was saying good
night at her doorway in the semiprivacy of the flickering
light of the hallway gas lamp. Minnie heard the whispered
rustle of their voices and although she despised herself for
doing it, she tiptoed out of bed and opened her hallway
door a tiny crack. She saw the ring going on Caroline's
finger, closed the door softly, and hurried back to bed.

"You can get your own breakfast in the morning," she muttered to her snoring husband. "I've earned a morning of
sleeping-in."

The wedding date was set for March, almost a year away.
It was a long wait but it was impossible to make it sooner.
Caroline had to make arrangements for care of her widowed
mother; Grandfather Snow, engineer on a seagoing tugboat
out of Boston harbor, had died with nothing left for support
of his family.

Big Sam needed time to get settled and arrange for a house.
He was now working for the Western Cooperage Company,
a mill and logging firm that was building a logging railroad
into virgin timber of the Klaskanine River basin south and
east of Astoria in Clatsop County. It was the start of an association that would last thirty-one years.

Logging was big business in the West by 1910. In British
Columbia alone that year there were 299 outfits with camps
and operations in the big timber. Fourteen thousand men
were on the payroll and they were aided in the job of hauling
out the big sticks by 353 steam donkey engines, 31 logging
locomotives, and 1770 horses.

Oil fuel to replace wood was being given a trial by some
of the more progressive operators. It was hotter, faster, and

easier to handle than wood and as it produced far fewer
sparks using it was one way to help reduce the risk of forest
fires. It had proven practical for locomotives but there still
were problems to be worked out in converting donkey
engines.

This, too, was the year that Merrill & Ring, a Washington
logging firm, bought a Lidgerwood skidder, a multiengined
monster mounted on railway trucks that could be pushed by
locomotives to waiting walls of fresh, green timber. A circular sweep of its tangle of blocks, steel cables, and rigging
could lay waste forty acres.

In the same year the Chapman Timber Company of Scappoose, Oregon, in the single month of June cut, hauled, and
dumped into the Columbia River eight million nine hundred
thousand board feet of timber. Trainloads of logs streaming
from woods to water passed within whistling distance of the
grave of Thomas McKay, Oregon trader, trapper, and ex-
plorer, stepson of Dr. John McLoughlin and builder of old
Fort Boise in Idaho. McKay died on his Scappoose farm during the winter of 1849-50.

The great trading and trapping days of the Hudson's Bay
Company were long gone and forgotten. Oregon and the
Far West were on the trail of bigger and more exciting
game—trees, a natural resource that unlike the pelt of the
beaver seemed destined to go on and on forever.

For the first time in the three hundred years since 1608
when eight artisans of Polish and Dutch extraction were
sent from England to Jamestown to set up sawmills for the
settlers in Virginia, mill and logging camp operators began
thinking about their men.

The Whitney Company up the Columbia River from
Astoria a dozen or so miles boasted some extraordinary facilities for that day. These included hot and cold water showers, a club room with magazines and a hundred book library,
electric lights and refrigeration powered by the camp's own

generator, a barber shop, and bunkhouses that slept eighteen men on iron-framed bunks with springs and mattresses.

In a camp such as the Whitney a man almost didn't need a wife. A man lived like a king and had only to pay a nominal fee for his meals.

But doing without Caroline never entered Big Sam's mind. There wasn't a day passed that he didn't think about her and ache with loneliness. His solace was work—grueling, muscle-bruising effort that some nights sent him tumbling into a sound sleep before he had time to get his clothes off.

"You trying to kill yourself, Sam?" Clarence O. (Daddy) Hoyt—a mustachioed donkey engineer with an abiding interest in whiskey, women, and friends, in the order listed—once asked.

In 1910 building a railroad, even a logging railroad that required none of the careful computations and grade and curve tolerances of the big main-line carriers, was no easy undertaking. There were no trucks and giant earth-moving machines to make cuts and build fills. Self-powered steam shovels on railroad trucks dug their way through terrain where the V-shaped cuts to carry the tracks weren't overly large. Donkey engines with drag lines and huge scrapers gnawed away at the big jobs. Dynamite and pickaxes and shovels powered by human muscle took care of rock and stump removal and an assortment of other jobs connected with railroad building.

Big Sam spent most of his time with the whining cables of the steam donkeys. The company logged as it built its railroad. As the big trees were felled to clear a path for the right of way they were dragged to the end of the rails by donkey engine and loaded on cars and hauled to the tidewater dump. From there they were floated to mills.

Near the end of July in 1910 a small sawmill was built near the proposed camp site; before there was even a roof over its head, it began cutting logs into ties and bridge timbers and lumber for the camp buildings.

On Sundays, the only day of rest, Big Sam spent hours sorting through the week's output of lumber selecting firm, straight pieces for the home he and Caroline would share. The best that he could find wasn't any too good. The mill's only job was to saw. It didn't plane or smooth the boards. A prospective camp resident took what he got and thanked his lucky star that it was free.

When it came time to build, company carpenters did the work. A family man had a limited choice of building sites— he could have his house on the right-hand side of the track or the left-hand side of the track. Each home and bunkhouse and storage shed was mounted on log skids so it could be easily dragged onto a railroad car and moved to a new camp location closer to the timber, whenever necessary. Everything was built uncomfortably close to the railroad tracks. A derailment could send the butt of a ten-foot Douglas fir smashing into a house.

As the time for the wedding approached Big Sam was assailed by doubts. In sober reflection he wondered how he could have been such a fool as to ask a woman he loved to share such a wild existence. He wished desperately he had taken more time to explain precisely what a logging camp out West really was. Both Caroline and his sister Minnie, he now suspected, had a logging camp pictured as somewhat similar to a small New England farm community with a store or two, a church, a meeting place, a school, and comfortable square homes with white picket fences.

The Western Cooperage Company camp was exactly the opposite. To reach it you traveled ten miles up Youngs Bay in a chugging little gasoline launch named the *Teddy Roosevelt*. It left Astoria around 8 A.M. each day and ended its run about noon at the tiny logging and farming center of Olney, which was located on Youngs River and named after Cyrus Olney, an Oregon territorial judge in the 1850s. From Olney, if you were lucky, you hitched a ride in the cab of a logging locomotive for the five-mile trip to the camp. If you were unlucky and missed a train, you walked.

The closest sidewalk, street, doctor, or man in a business suit was in Astoria. The closest grocery store was the one owned by Fred Olson at Olney where he also operated a twenty-five-room hotel and a blacksmith shop. At best, it was a five-mile one-way hike for a sack of beans, a packet of needles, or a spool of thread.

Another thing that worried Big Sam was logging camp atmosphere. In Boston, Caroline worked for C. F. Hovey, next to the old-line firm of Jordan Marsh. C. F. Hovey, in later years bought out by Jordan Marsh, was a stationery store specializing in quality goods—proper calling cards, notepaper, and other Bostonian essentials. Each workday at C. F. Hovey passed in a cultivated atmosphere of polite and proper, softly spoken English, clean fingernails, scrubbed elbows, and polished shoes.

In the Western Cooperage Company's Olney camp each day started with a fresh mouthful of snoose or chewing tobacco, the roaring bellows of cursing men, and fire-breathing machines. Footwear were scuffed, leather-laced logging shoes with soles armed by rows of needle-sharp steel calks that cut into wood and bark like miniature ice picks and kept a man rooted firmly and safely to anything except water or rock.

The business suit in a logging camp was a pair of overalls held up by wide-strap suspenders and chopped off at the bottoms to eliminate the danger of a low-hanging pants leg catching on a limb or bush and pitching a man in front of a moving log or into a nest of lethal rigging.

It was a place where you ended the day either covered with mud and rain or dust and sweat. It was a place where you could leave a five dollar bill on the top of your bunk for weeks on end and no one would think of touching it; and where, on the job, your very best friend might yell out in a rage at you: "You dumb sonofabitch set that block on that

other stump and get your ass the hell out of the way. It's
time the logs were movin'."

Would Caroline understand a way of life so foreign to anything she had ever known? It was January 1911. Big Sam
was standing on a stump watching a turn of logs grind its
way through brush and mud toward the straining donkey
engine. A mixture of rain and snow swirled around his
weather-seamed face and bare head. In another month he
would head East for the wedding. Big Sam was wringing wet
but not only from the rain and snow. His pores were wide
open and he was sweating.

Using a Waterman's pen with a medium point and black
ink, Caroline Snow recorded in her wedding book that she
and her husband Samuel Job Churchill would be at home
"after June fifteenth at Western Cooperage Company's
Camp, Olney, Oregon."

The same book reveals that the couple was married March
15, 1911, in East Boston by the Reverend Wilbur G. Chaffee
with the bride's mother, Mrs. Clara E. Snow, and the groom's
sister, Mrs. S. P. Crouse, as witnesses. It was a small wedding
in the Snow living room and with less than two dozen members of the immediate families present.

Looking over the stock of wedding gifts, Big Sam found
himself wondering where they would all fit in his one-room,
twelve by twenty foot house. There was a bone-handled
carving set with a cut glass rest from the Stitch and Talk
Club; a cut glass spoon tray from a William Reed; a full
table setting of sterling silver including salt and pepper shakers; several pieces of tissue thin china; a silver tea set from
Marshall; a large mantel clock from a Portland, Oregon,
jewelry store; and the usual doilies, sofa pillows, lace table-
cloths, bedding, and other items.

"Just tell the company that by God you need a bigger
house," chuckled Marshall.

It was on a June day three months after their marriage that
a creaking railroad handcar heaped high with household

goods and honeymoon items came clattering into the Western Cooperage camp. Squeezed in among the swaying cargo and frantically reaching for slithering pots and pans that seemed determined to escape the little car and go bounding off in the brush and weeds that lined the railroad tracks, was Big Sam Churchill's busy bride—Caroline Snow Churchill.

Braking the car to a stop and anchoring it in place on the slight grade by shoving a piece of wood under one wheel, Big Sam eyed the little unpainted shack nailed together from rough-cut lumber and mounted on log skids. It looked smaller, meaner, and more untidy than ever.

Masking his uneasiness, he cradled his wife's ninety-two pounds in one arm and some honeymoon luggage in the other. "Caroline," he announced in a rumble of sound that was about as close as Big Sam could get to a whisper, "this is home."

Nestled in the crook of her husband's arm and with one of her arms around his neck, Big Sam's Bride from Boston carefully studied the exterior of the little house that was her first home of her own.

"Sam," she said, "it's perfect. There's only one thing we need to do. Before we even unpack let's go down to a store and buy some curtains to hide the bareness of the windows."

## Chapter 4

## PICKLES AND ICE CREAM

Mother was no more than settled in her logging camp home when a strange malady began making life miserable for her. It was a morning sickness that always seemed to come after Dad had gone to work and was over by noon. She ate less breakfast on the hunch that the sizable intake of food so early in the morning was upsetting her system. It made no difference. She still ended up sick. She eliminated breakfast entirely and was sicker than ever. She boiled the creek water that was used by everyone in the camp but it made no difference. She switched from coffee to tea and felt a little better but was still sick.

Frightened and unnerved, she finally told Dad. She had been suffering several days now and the situation was not improving. Dad thought maybe it was the adjustment to marriage that had possibly caused the trouble. He ordered a dose of salts and a day in bed. Salts as a cathartic was a logging camp home remedy for everything from measles to mumps to a sprained wrist. They only made Mother sicker.

The nearest doctor was in the town of Astoria, only fifteen miles away but still a half-day's trip by logging train and launch or plank and mud road. In desperation he sought the advice of the only other wife in camp. She was a Mrs. Kneeland. She listened intently to Dad's description of Mother's symptoms.

"It's nothing to be alarmed about," she assured Dad. "I'll take a look at her first thing in the morning." After Dad thanked her and left, Mrs. Kneeland turned to her husband. "That poor little Boston girl," she said.

"What's the matter with her?" asked her husband.

"I don't know yet for sure," said Mrs. Kneeland, "but I think she's pregnant."

One look at Mother the next morning and Mrs. Kneeland knew her suspicion of the night before was correct. Later in the morning after Mother's stomach had gotten control of itself, Mrs. Kneeland gave her the acid test.

"Caroline," she said, "how would you like a dish of ice cream and a pickle?"

Mother almost swooned in ecstacy. "I'd love it."

"Ice cream is out of the question," said Mrs. Kneeland, "but I've got some of Northwest Oregon's finest dilled cucumber pickles." She then told Mother what her problem was.

"Good heavens," choked Mother, "do you mean I'm going to have a little Sam?"

"As near as I can calculate from what you tell me, you have until the first part of December."

"But we were only married last March," said mother.

"You didn't waste any time," agreed Mrs. Kneeland. "Maine's a darn poor place to go on a honeymoon in winter. The cold makes you hate to get out of bed."

When Mother broke the news to Dad that night he was relieved but worried. "We'll have to put a lean-to addition on the house," he said, "and get you to a hospital."

Mother reminded him it was only July. He could relax awhile longer.

The days between July and December were busy ones for Mother. Mail came to the camp twice a week. Arrival of the precious pouches brought letters, cards, and more wedding gifts from the East. They also brought magazines and newspapers which Mother read page by page. In between mail days she wrote long letters describing life in a logging camp. Dad's early fears were groundless. She was fascinated by this towering world of trees, mountains, and almost utter silence at night, after the great machines were at rest.

With box camera and film she followed Dad into the woods for pictures of logging crews at work. In another day under different conditions she might well have become a chronicler with film and the written word of early logging days in Oregon. But what she did she did strictly as an amateur, prompted by sheer love of this vast outdoors and the man with open-collared shirt and voice of thunder who had brought her to it. Dozens of her pictures and letter accounts were sent to friends and relatives in the East. A few dozen pictures of her early life in the camp were preserved in an album.

Memories of that other world she had left behind doubtless returned at times to sadden and depress her. Whenever the memory patterns began asserting themselves at too frequent intervals she would stuff a few things in a paper sack, climb into the hot, steam-sizzling cab of a logging locomotive, and ride the five miles down to where the tracks crossed the buggy road from Astoria to Olney. From there it was a mile or so walk to Fred Olson's hotel and store. At the hotel she would enjoy the luxury of a fifty cent room and one of Mrs. Olson's superb twenty-five cent meals that included everything from meat and potatoes to homemade pies as well as snacks to munch on between meals.

In addition to watching the *Teddy Roosevelt* pull in to the dock and tie up on its arrival from Astoria there was the Olson general store to explore. And there was Mrs. Olson to confide in. She was a plump, jolly Finnish woman who never strayed more than a hundred yards from a simmering coffee pot. "There's one woman," Dad used to say of Mrs. Olson, "who can keep a secret longer than the person who told it to her."

As mum as a Catholic priest after confession, she carried with her to her grave thirty years of Western Cooperage household secrets by the time she passed away.

Olson's general store was like nothing Mother had ever seen. As it was the only store of any kind for ten miles around, its shelves were packed with everything from lamp and lantern wicks to patent medicines, from yardage goods for dresses to wagon repair parts and saddles. After the shelves, the walls, and the floor were filled with merchandise, dozens more items were hung from ropes and wires dangling from the ceiling.

Today a few rotted pilings and the remains of one building are all that are left of the Olney community. Milton (Buck) Olson, a young boy when Mother moved to the camp from Boston, operates a small sawmill in the area and for years maintained the old home place as a dairy. A tourist, slightly off the beaten track, and hustling along the black-topped route of State Highway 202 from Astoria into the Coast Range, would notice only a pasture-like area with evergreen blackberry vines threatening to engulf the entire area.

But Buck and I remember it as a metropolis more exciting than Astoria, or even Portland, where loggers in snagged pants and calked shoes crunched along the wooden plank sidewalks. A place where if you didn't beg but could eye the tilted jars of hard candy with just the right amount of longing, it was practically a leadpipe cinch that Mrs. Olson would lift the big glass cover off one of them, dip out a heaping hand-ful of the precious goodies, and hold out her hand with the magic words: "Say, I'll bet here's a boy who just hates candy."

Or she might usher you into the big, spotless kitchen of the hotel where the wood floors were scrubbed with hot lye water each afternoon and you could put a white glove on the top of the overworked wood range almost without picking up a grease spot.

It seemed no matter what time of day or night you arrived in Olney, Mrs. Olson was just about to take a batch of pies out of the oven. Sometimes they would be big overweight apple pies that weighed almost as much as a pair of logger's shoes. Or maybe it would be pumpkin or wild blackberry in summer, or huckleberry in the fall.

When Mrs. Olson served a small boy a piece of pie he was almost certain to weigh at least two pounds more when he finished than when he had started. "You can't grow on an empty stomach," she used to say. She felt the same way about loggers, many of whom were nothing more than overgrown boys at heart. No logger going to or from any of the many camps that sprang up in the region and along the Western Cooperage logging railroad ever went hungry or was without a place to sleep once he arrived at Mrs. Olson's hotel.

There was always a room and a bed and a meal for friend, foe, or stranger. A logger without funds was told to "Put a dollar in an envelope some day and address it Mrs. Olson, Olney, Oregon. I'll get it."

There would be no way of accurately checking to find out how much Mrs. Olson lost because of her generosity at the hotel but about the only ones who didn't pay were those who died with their boots on while getting logs from forest to mill. Death in a logging camp was usually brutal but quick. There were many ways for a man to die—under a rolling log, in a tangle of flying rigging and chokers, from the kickback of a giant tree as it toppled forward from its stump, from falling limbs plummeting to the ground from the top of a Douglas fir tree. These limbs, often twice the diameter of a man's thigh and weighing from fifty to two hundred pounds, would strike like lightning and at unexpected times. They might have been broken off months before in a storm or by a falling tree and lain there harmlessly hidden from view and precariously balanced until a wind or the tremors of ax and saw on the trunk below jarred them loose.

Their lethal descent could be almost soundless. The slight rustle of sound as they broke free and plunged toward the ground would usually be drowned by the noises of cutting crews, the staccato bark of steam donkey engines, the yells of head riggers calling out signals to a whistle punk who by jerking a wire which in turn activated a steam whistle would relay the orders to the donkey engineer.

But the most dangerous work in the woods was on the rigging, the type of work Dad did. An ordinary main-line cable used to drag in the logs would weigh two and a half pounds to the foot and feel as rigid as a steel bar when lying idle on the ground. But working on a highlead rig as I did in the late 1930s I've watched one of these writhing snakes of steel whip out like a fisherman's fly line severing small trees or anything else unlucky enough to be in its way.

Everything in a logging operation, even in my father's day, had weight—terrible weight. So simple a thing as an ax weighed from three to five and a half pounds, steel-sheathed pulleys (called blocks in a logging camp) to guide the lashing, straining lines ranged from eighty pounds to more than a ton in weight. A dragline scoop, or grader, used in making cuts and fills and for other chores in railroad right of way construction, would tip the scales at two and a half tons for the larger models. A simple, high-speed yarding engine used to drag in the logs was a spitting, roaring thirty tons of steel and steam; mounted on its hewn-log sled, so it could pull itself by its own strength over mountainous ridge or across a boulder-strewn canyon, it would weigh a good forty tons.

As the days of her pregnancy lengthened Mother worried more and more about Dad and the daily risks he and the others faced. It became a macabre ritual: she walked to the crew train each morning with Dad to see him off to work and was there each night when the train pulled into camp to make certain, early, that he was arriving home safe.

It wasn't until Mrs. Kneeland took command that this gnawing horror of the imminence of death was corralled and driven back into its proper perspective.

"If you want to see Big Sam dead keep doing what you're doing," she railed at Mother one day in a fit of rage that was rare for her. Her sudden outburst sent Mother into a sudden spasm of tears. Mrs. Kneeland needled and needled and the tears flowed harder.

After Mother had regained some of her composure and started returning volley for volley, Mrs. Kneeland eased up and smiled. "You'll be fine now," she promised. "A woman carrying a child sometimes lets her mind do strange things with her. A good cry eases tensions."

She then told Mother that men like Dad need an uncluttered mind and razor-sharp reflexes to stay alive. "You weren't helping one bit acting like a Boston girl," she chided. A few days later, Dad, no more than flicked by a steel cable, was sent sprawling head over ankles against a stump and worked the rest of the day with two broken ribs. In full charge of her emotions, thanks to Mrs. Kneeland, Mother wasted no time with fears and tears when he came grunting up the length of plank that served as a walk between the railroad track and our house. She peeled off his shirt and eased him out of the upper half of his long wool underwear. She studied the ugly bruises and abrasion marks left by the cable, then carefully cleansed them with soap and warm water and alcohol. Ordering Dad to exhale, she then wrapped his ribcage in a corset of clean sheet torn into a long wide strip. Safety pins held it firm and in place.

Mrs. Kneeland, standing by to guide and supervise, pronounced the job excellent. Mother was pleased and confident. "Any more broken bones and I'll have to place you on report," she warned Dad sternly, mocking the disciplinary tones she had put up with for so many years at C. F. Hovey's.

Mrs. Kneeland placed an arm around Mother's shoulders. "Welcome to the club," she smiled. "I now declare you a full-fledged logger's wife capable of childbirth, bone mending, and worthy of the respect of all other wives." At this point Mother and Mrs. Kneeland were still the only two women in camp. A timber faller had fixed up a tent as a honeymoon home for his bride but she hadn't arrived from Sweden yet.

It was also about this time that I was beginning to be a problem. "Samuel feels like a bucket of lead," Mother complained one day to Dad. "If December doesn't hurry up I'll weigh more than one of your steam donkey engines."

Throughout these early months of pregnancy both Mother and Dad always referred to me as a boy and my name was Samuel. Mother's older sister, married and living in Boston, hinted in one of her letters that the Good Lord might have other ideas. Maybe I would turn out to be a girl. Mother was indignant in her reply. "When I get up mornings," she wrote, "I know I've been in bed with a man." She went on to say that it was inconceivable that Big Sam would sire anything but a male.

A week before my estimated arrival time Dad and Mother rode the logging train down to Olney and boarded the *Teddy Roosevelt* for the boat trip to Astoria. He checked Mother into St. Mary's Hospital, modernized and still in business in 1964, and made all other arrangements. Dr. O. B. Estes, an old-line Astoria physician whose grandsons became very close friends of mine in later years, was Mother's doctor.

The afternoon of December 5, 1911, Dr. Estes sent word out to the Western Cooperage camp that Dad better be showing up. I was expected within the next day or two. With a few hours sleep Dad could face or handle virtually any emergency. It was too late to catch the launch from Olney to Astoria and he wouldn't think of asking someone to drive him in by horse and wagon over the rough ten miles of mud and plank road between Olney and Astoria.

He solved the problem with his usual good judgment and calm. He set the alarm for midnight and crawled into bed right after supper. When the alarm went off he dressed in his work clothes and logging shoes, rolled his suit, a clean white shirt, tie, dress socks, and shoes in a watertight slicker, and started hiking. It was a damp, misty night but one that was ideal for a man used to the outdoors setting out on a fifteen-mile hike before breakfast.

For leg muscles conditioned by years of leaping from log to log, and plowing through underbrush and over windfalls on hillsides and in canyons, a little old walk of fifteen miles was a restful vacation.

In a little more than four hours Big Sam had covered the fifteen miles from camp to the Astoria Sixteenth Street city limits on the south slope of Coxcomb Hill. The steel calks in the soles of his logging boots kicked up angry little sparks as he strode rapidly along the paved surface of the narrow, steep, crooked road that was called a street and wound toward the crest of the hill. At the top of the hill, with the broad lap of the Columbia River camouflaged in darkness below him and the diffused lights of the little town peering up at him through a dribble of rain and mist, he ducked into a roadside path that led into the brush. Shivering in the predawn cold he slipped out of his logging clothes and into his suit and dress shoes. He rolled his logging duds into the same watertight slicker that minutes before had protected his dress clothes. With the bundle under one arm he followed the path back out to the street and continued his hike down the river side of the hill and into town. It was 5:45 A.M., four hours and forty-five minutes since he started out from the camp.

The lobby of St. Mary's Hospital was deserted when he entered except for one nurse behind a desk labeled "Emergency." He considered a moment and decided that a man who had walked fifteen miles and was about to become a father might be entitled to emergency status. The nurse told him they were getting ready to take his wife to the delivery room. He had arrived in the nick of time. Big Sam sprinted up a flight or two of stairs to Caroline's room. She looked wan, in pain, and frightened. He walked over and tucked one of her perspiring hands in his. She opened her eyes and when she saw who it was the tight little fist relaxed, the fear faded from her face. "I told Dr. Estes my Big Sam would be here," she smiled. "Now you go get some rest while I bring you a son."

## Chapter 5

# DON'T ROCK THE BOAT

It wasn't until I was twenty-five years of age, working in the camp and living in the same bunkhouse as Dad, that I learned I was no great shakes as a baby. He admitted it in answer to a direct question from me during one of the numerous evening talks we used to have about the old days and his and Mother's early life.

I arrived at 7:30 A.M., December 6, 1911, after persistent effort on the part of Dr. Estes. The Astoria *Daily Budget* made passing mention of the event in its December 6 issue: "At St. Mary's Hospital today a fine boy was born to the wife of Samuel Churchill of Olney, Ore."

"They's two times a man is almost certain to get his name in a paper," mused Big Sam, "when he's born and when he dies." Apparently Dad had a few doubts about me during my first few hours of life. I weighed six and a quarter pounds and was twenty-one inches long at birth, neither of which was impressive information to take back to camp. My first tooth made its appearance, according to the very detailed record of my arrival and statistics in Mother's handwriting in my baby book, on November 16, 1912. My first spoken words were "chair" and "cow," to quote Mother.

Rearing an infant in a logging camp, miles from the nearest doctor, drug store, and hot and cold water tap, was not an easy task, even for wives who had already accomplished the feat a time or two.

Mother was totally helpless in the face of such emergencies as colic, rashes, diaper changing, burping, and other routine matters in baby handling. Mrs. Kneeland was appalled that a grown woman could be so ignorant. "For heaven's sake, Caroline," she once said to Mother, "don't they have babies in Boston?"

In recent weeks the camp's population of married women had increased slightly. There was Mrs. Guy Lillich who taught Mother the fine points of burping a baby and changing its diapers. Mrs. Kneeland was on twenty-four-hour call for such things as colic and other upsets. The little bride from Sweden had arrived and was honeymooning in her tent but she was of little or no help—she hadn't yet learned to speak English.

When Mother was on the verge of complete disintegration and ready to demand a complete course in motherhood at the hospital, there was Mrs. Olson or Emma Holm. Mrs. Olson, naturally, could burp a baby with one hand and prepare an evening meal for twenty-five boarders with the other. Emma, a teenager, was the daughter of a pioneer Olney rancher and dairyman, John Holm. In an emergency she'd walk the two miles from the Holm farm to the Western Cooperage camp and get me bathed, cleaned, and smiling while Mother would relax with a book or magazine.

Still living in the same general area, Emma is married to Ernest Splester, a man who worked with Big Sam for many years. Whenever I'm back in the old camp area I head for her house as eagerly as Mother used to. The coffee pot is always on the stove and a new story about Mother and Dad always seems to come to light as we sip the hot, black liquid from brimful cups.

Back in 1911 doctors were less eager to get their patients on their feet and doing things after childbirth or an operation. Mother, for example, remained in the hospital two weeks after I was born, resting and building up strength. When it came time to return to the camp Dad came to Astoria and they boarded the *Teddy Roosevelt* together. A brisk wind was kicking out of the southwest and the surfaces of the

1. Big Sam, perched second from the left, with some of the other men who brought logs this size out of the forests of Oregon in the early 1900s.

2. A giant Douglas fir, the undercut already in place, towers over the man at the right of its base in the dense forests of the early logging days. *(Kenneth Long Photo)*

3. A typical logging camp in the early 1920s—this one near Silverton, Oregon. *(Kenneth Long Photo)*

4. Big Sam's bride, Caroline Snow Churchill.

5. The launch *Teddy Roosevelt*, which brought Big Sam and his bride from Astoria to their new logging camp home.

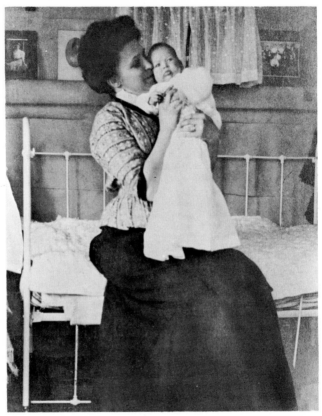

6. Big Sam's wife and son.

Columbia River and Youngs Bay roiled into a foamy chop that set the little boat to rolling and bouncing the moment it left the dock.

It took me all of ten minutes to get seasick. An old sea hand—my Grandfather Snow, remember, was engineer on a seagoing tugboat out of Boston Harbor—Mother could ride out any kind of a storm. But she was worried about me and Dad was looking a little green around the gills. She made her way to the pilot house and told the pilot: "I wish you'd stop rocking this boat. My baby's sick and my husband is at the railing."

The pilot stared at her in open-mouthed astonishment. If Mother had been a man he would have known exactly what to do. But there she was, a mite of a woman with sparks dancing in her eyes and a baby in her arms. The pilot seemed to be chewing over one word after another and discarding them one by one as ungentlemanly and unsuited for this quaint but frustrating occasion. In desperation he finally blurted: "Lady, if you can do any better you just step over here and take ahold of this wheel." To his consternation and surprise Mother did exactly as he directed and as a bonus deposited me, slobbering and regurgitating, in his arms. With an easy flip of the wheel she brought the little boat around a point or two and miraculously smoothed out the ride.

"Get her out of the troughs and up on the sides and tops of the swells and she'll handle and ride better," Mother explained with a glance to see that I was safe and not dangling by my feet or in some other unapproved position. "Keep her headed dead ahead for Green Mountain and she'll ride out this little chop as smoothly as a baby buggy rolling across a carpet," Mother told him. The pilot could no longer contain himself. Handing me back to Mother, he took back the wheel, steered straight for Green Mountain, and in a dumfounded tone that shook trees and piling on both sides of the bay, bellowed: "Holy Jesus jumped up Christ!"

With the boat running smoother, in less than half an hour

Dad and I were feeling better. It wasn't until weeks later, after the pilot had spread the story in Olney and every saloon in Astoria, that Dad was aware of what Mother had done. "Caroline," he asked one night at supper, "where did you ever learn to steer a boat?"

"Up until my father died I spent more hours going in and out of Boston Harbor on a tugboat than I spent on the streets of Boston," she said. I don't know whether or not it had any significance but from that time on Dad always called Mother "Carrie" instead of "Caroline."

And when Mother was having problems with me and diapers and colic, he came to her rescue by reminding Mrs. Kneeland and the others that maybe Mother didn't know much about babies but she knew more than any fool land-lubber in camp about boats.

Although Dad had planned on adding a lean-to bedroom to our house he delayed the project when I arrived because the camp was going to be moved. The railroad building pro-gram had progressed another five miles up the canyon of the south fork of the Klaskanine River (we called it Creek) and the camp would be designated a headquarters camp, moved to the new location, and remain there permanently. The new location would be ten miles from Olney but at a spot where the railroad crossed the county road. Although it was more isolated in terms of distance, proximity to the county road was an improvement.

By present standards it wasn't much of a road. From Astoria to Olney it bordered the tide flats of Youngs Bay for several miles and was within eyereach of the water for all but a mile or two of the ten-mile route. Where the earth was firm, the road was dirt. Where it was soggy, rock ballast was used sparingly. The worst spots were planked. Step off the planks and you might end up waist-deep in mire.

But from Olney past the new Western Cooperage camp site and on over a false crest of the Coast Range into the Nehalem Valley and the tiny lumbering community of

Jewell the road passed through virgin country. Here was a forest primeval such as man on this earth is never again likely to see except in the deep interior of Washington State's Olympic Peninsula. Here was a region of lush growth and shadowed splendor untouched by ax or saw where the road builders found it faster and less costly to squeeze the road between the hips of giant trees rather than attempt to clear a right of way by falling them.

In summer you walked or rode a meandering route punctured at intervals by shafts of sunlight. In winter the weaving canopy of green protected you from direct assault of wind and rain but managed to soak you never the less with stored-up deluges that would come cascading down from the mist-shrouded tops.

But to a handful of people whose main lifeline to the outside world for more than a year had been the creaky ties and steel of a logging railroad and the spray-coated deck of a tiny gasoline launch a road of any kind at its doorstep was the ultimate in convenience and progress.

In a letter to members of the East Boston Stitch and Talk Club, Mother predicted, a little sadly, that the road would doubtless open up the country. She loved this wild, reckless country and since she had been one of the first married women in camp, regarded the Western Cooperage Company, its employees, and the timbered vastness in which they lived and worked as part of her own personal domain.

"I would rather visit the outside world at my pleasure than have the outside world trampling over this unspoiled beauty of Big Sam's land," she wrote to an East Boston friend, Anne Deering.

She also expressed concern over what improved roads and other transporation methods might do to the future of the *Teddy Roosevelt*. "It's such a friendly, happy little craft and so loyal," she said in another letter, "I would be heartsick were it to go."

Her fears were well founded. Improved roads and the

building of the Western Cooperage Company camps and railroad did open up the country to new faces and new battle
fronts from which new battalions of men and machines
launched greedy attacks against the defenseless line of retreating timber.

But the little *Teddy Roosevelt* didn't give up easily. It continued its Astoria to Olney run and return for many more
years. Mother rode it frequently, even after the roads were
widened and graveled and horse-drawn vehicles were being replaced by automobiles.

"It was here when I needed it," she used to say of the
*Teddy Roosevelt*, "and I'll continue to patronize it whenever
I can."

## Chapter 6

## CLAM CHOWDER AND BEANS

Establishment of the Western Cooperage headquarters camp at its new and permanent location was one of two major events for us during the winter of 1912–13. One was that we moved from the camp for a time while Dad worked for the company in some of its mill operations at St. Johns, a suburb of Portland, and at Trenholm, a deep-woods community near St. Helens. The second was Uncle Marshall's marriage.

"Thank heavens," said Mother when she heard the news.

"Now he'll settle down," predicted Dad.

"I pity any woman married to that free-spending hell raiser," was the comment of most of the other wives in the camp.

Aunt Blanche was a western girl and when she and Uncle Marsh came to the camp after their marriage everyone agreed wholeheartedly that he sure was going to spend the winter snuggled up to a real looker.

"Don't these people think of anything but sex?" Mother asked Mrs. Johnson, a pipe-smoking resident who lived in a homemade house of hand-split cedar shakes back from the railroad track on the bank of Klaskanine Creek.

"By heaven, Caroline," warned Mrs. Johnson, using a broom to flick some dirt from the piece of hewn log that served as a step up to the kitchen entrance of her house, "don't you go a tryin' to change too many things around here."

She doubtless was remembering Mother's earnest but ill-fated effort to interest Western Cooperage housewives in New England cookery. Logging camp fare was partial to hot cakes, hot mush, and pork for breakfast. Other favorites for other meals were venison roasts and steaks, from deer shot in or out of season; bear meat late in the fall when the animals were fat from loading up on grubs, wild honey, huckleberries, and wild blackberries. There was also an abundance of grouse and other game birds as well as domestic beef and lamb. These along with dark, thick meat gravies, boiled potatoes, boiled white beans, carrots, cabbage, and turnips were part of the basic daily menu in most logging camp homes. A working logger such as Dad could usually handle around nine thousand calories a day of hearty foods including ample servings of pie, cake, cookies, homemade breads and other delicacies.

Since they had both been born and reared in New England Mother and Dad had a particular fondness for sea foods, chowders, stews, soups, and especially Boston baked beans. Dad adored Mother's Boston baked beans, cooked slowly in a special crockery pot brought out from Boston. He could almost drink her rich, carefully seasoned and textured gravies. Her knack at cooking and seasoning wild game or a beef or lamb roast made eating both a physical and a spiritual pleasure.

In a society where a wife's social stature depended to a great extent on her ability to turn out mouth-watering cuisine over a wood-burning cookstove, Mother was at the top, standing shoulder to shoulder with such acknowledged artists as Mrs. Olson, Mrs. Kneeland, and Mrs. Lillich. She had one failing—salads. When lettuce or other greens were not available she'd often send me on scouting trips along the banks of Klaskanine Creek in search of water cress and other natural greens. Greens, Mother contended, were nature's body conditioners. Among other things they kept you moving on schedule to the outhouse, kept your blood pure, and your eyes bright.

Dad was violently opposed to salads and leafy foods, especially creekside wild greens, and the rest of the camp supported his stand.

Mrs. Johnson happened in one evening just as Dad was sitting down to a snack of what he liked to refer to for Mother's benefit as "leaves and grasses." Mrs. Johnson stared at the heaping dish of greens garnished with slices of fresh tomato and cucumber topped with mayonnaise. Her face mirrored utter disgust. Ignoring Dad, she turned to Mother.

"How do you expect a man to work and raise a family on stuff like that?" she almost shouted at Mother.

"He's had a meal of roast beef, potatoes, gravy, and pie for dessert," said Mother, trying to keep a grip on her temper. "And remember, the human body needs roughage."

"In a pig's ass it does," Mrs. Johnson snapped back. Mother was out of her chair as though she had just sat on the business end of a hat pin. Mother classified cuss words into "normal profanity" and "vulgar profanity." The word Mrs. Johnson had just used was one of those Mother despised. Wordlessly and with the color blanched from her face, she propelled Mrs. Johnson toward the door. Dad gave the table a slap with the flat of his hand that sent the lamp chimney bouncing out of its holder. It hit the table with a shatter of glass. The plate of salad tilted, and lettuce, cucumber, and tomato went slithering. The silver salt and pepper shakers that were wedding presents bounced like two tennis balls. Mother and Mrs. Johnson skidded to a stop.

"Clean up this mess," Dad told Mother, motioning toward the table. Then taking Mrs. Johnson by the arm he led her out of the house and down the path that ran through the underbrush between our house and her house. Mr. Johnson, dressed in long underwear and a clean pair of overalls, was sitting on the hewn-log step of his house airing himself when Dad and Mrs. Johnson came bursting from the path into the little clearing surrounding the house.

"Johnson," Dad said quietly but firmly, "I'll be much

obliged if you see fit to keep your fool woman locked up the rest of the night."

In later years Mr. Johnson told me the brusque request aroused his curiosity but one look at Dad and it didn't seem an especially good time to start asking him questions.

It had taken less than five minutes to escort Mrs. Johnson to her home and return to our house but by the time Dad was back Mother had the table in order and a spare chimney in the lamp. Where the salad dish had been there was now a healthy portion of cold roast beef, warmed-over spuds and gravy, and a fifteen-hundred-calorie serving of deep apple pie.

Dad sat down at the table without a word or a glance at Mother. He hitched his chair into place, bowed his head as though he were about to ask the blessing. Cocking his head a little to one side and looking square at Mother, he said: "Who do I thank for this? The Good Lord or that filthy-mouthed Mrs. Johnson?"

During the time we were living in St. Johns and Trenholm, the camp had grown tremendously. It was now a community of almost one hundred persons including two dozen youngsters many of whom were in my age bracket. Camp buildings now included a one-room school house with between eight and ten pupils ranging in age from first to eighth graders and taught by one teacher. In addition to the old original line of houses on each side of the railroad track homes were now scattered along the county road and down along the creek below where the Johnsons lived. Up the track a few hundred feet from the residential area of the camp were the blacksmith and machine shops for repair of railroad rolling stock and logging equipment; office quarters; cookhouse and dining room for the single men; and an area of bunkhouses, some of which were mounted on railroad cars and strung out end to end on a couple of special railroad sidings.

Mounted on railroad cars, as they were, they could be quickly and easily moved by locomotives to locations handier to the logging areas as the timber line fell back farther and farther from the permanent spot of the headquarters camp.

Office and shop employees, locomotive crews, and married men with families lived at the headquarters camp. A crew train transported the married men and single men who lived at the main camp but worked with the logging engines to their woods' jobs and back each day. Three miles from our camp and deeper into the Klaskanine River basin the company established what it called Camp 2. This was a bachelor camp with bunkhouses and a cookhouse. A visit to Camp 2 was always anticipated with tingling excitement by us boys and girls living at the main camp. At Camp 2 you could load up with cookies from the cookhouse, sit peacefully in the sunshine with your feet and legs dangling over the side of a big stump, and watch a half-dozen thundering steam donkey engines and their crews at work.

A lad with sharp ears might hear the booming voice of his own father above the constant cacophony of shouted signals, orders, chattering donkey engine whistles and slap and whine of straining blocks and cables. A good pair of eyes might give you a glimpse of the man you worshiped even above God. He might be racing full tilt along a log, leaping clear of a threshing cable, or dodging a flying limb or sapling.

But the most precious moments of all were when your mother would take you right out beside one of the giant, thunder-voiced machines mounted on its monstrous log sled. You'd have to shout to make yourself heard above the roaring inferno inside the monster's firebox, the screeching directives to the engineer from the boiler-mounted steam whistle, and the lumbering groans from the huge steam-powered drums as they reeled in or slacked off the tons of arm-thick cables.

And if your mother really loved you she'd plan far enough ahead so that you'd have your own lunch in your own lunch bucket and when the noon whistle blew you would eat lunch with the crew.

With the big machine at rest and quiet except for the sput-
tering sounds of escaping steam and noontime grunts of
idling flame in the firebox you no longer had to shout and
could talk in normal tones. As the men hurried in toward the
donkey engine someone might shout: "Hey, Sam, hurry up.
They's a young fella here hungry as all get out."

And then there he would be. The man you loved above
all others. A man with sweat and grime trickling down his
face. A man so tall you had to tilt your head way back to
look up at his face. A man who carried with him the rich,
clean smell of freshly cut fir and hemlock timber and the
heady, perfume-like odor of pitch. And maybe he'd reach
down and with his two powerful hands sweep you and your
lunch bucket off the ground and onto the donkey engine sled.
And he'd do the same with your mother. And with the agility
of a cat he'd make an effortless leap and join you. The calks
that studded the soles of his logging work shoes would cut
into the bare wood of the sled. The crunching noise they
made as they dug in had a firm, safe sound. At that moment
you were tired of being a boy. You wished a Good Fairy,
as in the books your mother read to you, would come along,
wave her magic wand, and turn you into a grown man just
like your dad with calk shoes, big hands, and dirt and sweat
on your face.

You knew each and every one of these men and you
adored them all. Hot-tempered, rough-talking, and capable
of blowing a month's pay on whiskey and women in a matter
of hours during a Saturday night in town, they always were
careful of their language around wives and young people.
And they always seemed to have time to answer questions
and not as though you were a boy but as though you were a
grown-up asking serious, thoughtful questions worthy of serious, thoughtful answers.

The amount of logging information stored in your head
was rather astonishing. Long before you learned how to con-
jugate a verb you knew how to roll a choker so as to

swing a log free of an obstruction. Even before you were old enough to go to school you knew the company's Humboldt yarders weighed almost fifty thousand pounds not including the weight of the log sled. You knew an eleven by thirteen special could reel in a log on good ground at better than four hundred feet a minute and send the rigging and chokers racing back into the woods at more than a thousand feet a minute.

You could read the whistle signals before you had learned how to read or write. You had a vague working knowledge of locomotives and the giant machine lathes in the machine shop before you were aware that Salem was the capital city of Oregon.

You never stopped to wonder how it was that you knew all these things so early in life. It was just part of the wonderful experience of growing up in a logging camp. You were proud and interested in the work your father did in the camp. You lived a part of his life each day. And you yearned for the day when you too would lace on a pair of calk shoes and leave your own special imprint alongside the footsteps of your father in the woods.

There were special enjoyments for boys and girls living in the Western Cooperage camp that those who lived in town were not likely to experience. One was in the person of Billy Deeds. I doubt if Billy Deeds had ever been east of the Cascade Range that ranged in a jumble of crags and snow-capped peaks from British Columbia to Northern California between the Rocky Mountains and the Pacific. But he had a New Englander's love for Mother's Boston baked beans, chowders, fish dishes, stews, and soups. When he wasn't on his swaying, bouncing, solid-tired old Mack truck covering the mail and inland delivery route between Astoria and Jewell, he was usually in our kitchen sniffing around for a New England cookbook handout.

We had barely gotten settled on our return to the camp after the time away at St. Johns and Trenholm when Billy

Deeds came knocking at the door. "Caroline," he beamed, using the back of one hand to tidy up a few stains of tobacco juice clinging to the corners of his mouth, "as soon as I seen those heaps of magazines, letters, and newspapers going into the Western Cooperage mail pouches I knowed you and Big Sam was back." On these neighborly little calls Billy would brazenly stare at the cookstove in hopes of being in time for a bowl of simmering stew, a fresh pot of Boston baked beans, oven-hot bread, or plump, golden brown doughnuts fresh from the big iron skillet filled with boiling hot cooking oil.

Next to munching on Mother's cooking Billy loved settling down in Dad's big wooden rocking chair and thumbing through the accumulation of magazines and newspapers and books that seemed always to find welcome refuge in our house. We subscribed to all of his favorite magazines of the day including *The American Magazine, National Geographic, The Saturday Evening Post, Atlantic Monthly,* and others.

While studying the contents of a magazine Billy maintained a steady stream of chatter about current events of the past few days along his delivery route. In a region where the only telephones in a thousand square miles were in Mrs. Olson's hotel at Olney and the headquarters camp office of the Western Cooperage, Billy Deeds provided an important and sought-after service. When Billy and his truck bounced into view on the mail trip from Astoria to Jewell a dozen camp wives would begin at fever pitch to hustle batches of fresh-baked rolls, pastries, and other oven delights from kitchen cookstoves. It was a brazen, premeditated plan of luring Billy into their homes for an early personal report on news, gossip, and tidbits of scandal he may have picked up along his route.

Billy knew what these news-hungry women in camp wanted and he delivered a well-rehearsed program of current events items spiced up with the latest gossip, rumors, and whispered morsels that he had heard, thought up, or dug up along his route. He was wise enough to let each woman make up her own mind as to what she wanted to accept as truth, rumor, or gossip. It would soon be repeated as fact. It was Mother who finally put a stop to the practice. On this particular day Billy stopped at our house first. He used to rotate the order of visitations so as not to show favoritism. He told Mother that a new little bride at one of the nearby camps had worked in a house of prostitution before she married and came to the camp to live.

"Billy," Mother asked, pinning him to Dad's rocking chair with a look as wicked as a barbed gaff hook, "do you know that to be true or is that just gossip?"

Billy squirmed and blustered but finally admitted it was gossip. "I think it's more than that," Mother said, impaling him with another icy glare. "I think you are spreading a dirty, vicious lie and if you so much as hint such a thing to anyone else you'll never again be welcome in this house." Billy promised to kill the rumor. As it turned out Mother was right. The little bride had a sexy look but she'd never even been near a house of ill repute. From then on Mother never quite trusted Billy Deeds and his news reports. She became a virtual censor and even went so far as to make him promise to eliminate gossip and rumors from his accounts of current events. Mother's insistence on truth took a lot of the fun and anticipation out of Billy's news reports. They became about as interesting as the legal notices in a newspaper. It finally reached a point where Billy could feel the interest of his former clientele dwindling. There were fewer hot rolls and pastry offerings coming out of camp ovens on mail days. Some of the wives didn't seem to care whether he stopped by for a news chat or not.

"Dammit, Caroline," he finally complained in fear and desperation to Mother, "there just ain't enough honest news to keep things excitin'. These people need a little gossip and spicy rumors to keep their interest up."

Mother had already decided that the promise to tell the

truth and nothing but the truth that she had extracted from Billy was a mistake. His arrival in camp on mail days was no longer the exciting event it had been when he was free to mix fact and fancy with a free hand and pass the whole kit and kaboodle off as truth. Billy was a born prevaricator, storyteller and showman. Restricting him to what he knew to be the truth was as cruel and pointless as fencing in a herd of deer or caging a bear.

She canceled the truth promise and Billy Deeds and the Western Cooperage camp lived again.

Even though Mother and Billy Deeds were the closest of friends there were occasions when she would not allow him in our house. Those were the times when he'd had a little too much booze. At such times the old truck would come weaving into camp with Billy rocking back and forth behind the wheel and singing at the top of his voice. His repertoire included everything from "Jingle Bells" to "The Farmer in the Dell" and "Yankee Doodle" to "Holy, Holy, Holy."

Mother used to have a fit when he'd sweep into "Holy, Holy, Holy." I've never heard anyone hit the part "Lord God Al-migh-ty" with the fervor, goodwill, volume, and off-tune beauty of Billy Deeds.

"It's sacrilegious," Mother used to complain to Dad. "Billy isn't himself. It isn't right to let him do that."

"They's not a mean or dishonest hair on Billy's head, drunk or sober," Dad would fire back, "and the Good Lord knows it." The rest of the camp agreed with Dad and in time Mother came around to their way of thinking.

Somehow, after you had been around him for a while, you just knew that with Billy Deeds whooping it up and keeping an eye on our part of the earth the Lord was free to work elsewhere. Maybe in Europe where there seemed to be a shortage of folks like Billy Deeds and armed men were already fighting.

## Chapter 7

## GOD IS EVERYWHERE

In the Western Cooperage camp there was no such thing as electricity, indoor plumbing, sidewalks, or street lights. Interior lighting was by kerosene lamp. A few families had gasoline lamps that used mantles and gave off a brilliant white light, but Dad and Mother distrusted gasoline as a fuel and so did most of the others in camp.

Outside illumination at night was tied directly to the barometer. The stars and the moon were our street lights. During periods of cloudy or overcast skies the nights would be pitch black. On summer nights with clear skies overhead we lived under a jeweled dome whose heavenly splendor seemed at treetop level. The stars on their own gave sufficient light to follow the narrow path through the underbrush from the house to the outdoor toilet. Or you could walk along the railroad track with a minimum risk of stumbling over the rock ballast between the ties and breaking your neck.

But it took a full-bosomed moon to bring out the full beauty God had implanted in this muscular, magnificently proportioned land. In the hard, unflattering light of the sun the camp looked to be exactly what it was—a dingy community of unpainted, weather-bleached homes, shops, bunkhouses, and storage buildings. Giant lifeless skeletons that once had been living trees, faded by wind, rain, and sun until they were almost white, haunted the hunting grounds of the great logging machines. In the light of day these towering sentinels of death and mass destruction seemed to watch silently over the millions of tons of shattered beauty in unwanted waste-trees left behind to rot and fester for decades to come on the gouged and abandoned land.

But on moonlight nights it was as though God had at last taken pity on this sick and weary land. And on the people who loved it but hadn't yet learned how to utilize and at the same time protect it. That time would come but it hadn't come yet.

In the soft, gray-white radiance of a moonlight night the harsh ugliness of the camp and the logged-over lands surrounding it was stroked away as though by some Old Master possessed with infinite patience, love and understanding and a magical brush. Often, on these very special and almost mystical nights, Mother who sometimes said her bedtime prayers outside with her face pointed up toward the stars would call out: "Sam, Samuel! Come out here and look. God in all His glory is looking down on the Western Cooperage camp tonight."

I doubt if my father could quote a single sentence from the Good Book. But he had an inborn feeling and respect for God. He lived by the Ten Commandments as naturally as though he had had a hand in their evolvement.

To both Dad and Mother God was as much a part of the Churchill family and its daily life as was I or Uncle Marsh. The fact that He was unseen was of no significance. The important thing was that He was there.

"God is everywhere," Mother used to tell me. "He's in the song of the robin and the chatter of a bluejay. He's in the dancing waters of Klaskanine Creek; the bloom of trilliums in the spring; the bark of a fir tree; the roots of a wild blackberry vine. He's in the dancing light of a little boy's eyes," she'd say, patting my head, "and in the hearts of men like your father."

It used to be great fun daydreaming incidents in which God would suddenly materialize alongside some member of our family. In these mental musings I was always calm, and God and I would chat about things such as the good-natured swearing of Jim Chester; where the best fishing holes in Klaskanine Creek were; and how I would someday punch that bully Phil Peets right square in the nose.

Mother, in my daydreams, always turned out a lovable woman in utter panic. She would drop pots and pans, burn things in the oven, and act so flustered that God would sometimes bend over in fits of laughter.

Dad was almost as calm as I was. He was so big and strong that even God was impressed. Sometimes we'd all be down at the crossing—where the logging railroad crossed the county road at the lower end of camp—on a Sunday afternoon, me and Dad and God and maybe a bunch of loafing loggers and some of the camp kids such as my close friend Rex Gaynor, the Cox boys, Fen and Jake Johnson, and maybe Helen Boyle, whom I kind of liked for a girl.

Right in front of everybody I'd ask God who was the stronger, my dad or Rex Gaynor's dad, Mike. God gave the nod to my dad every time. In these childhood flights of fancy God backed me up in everything I said and believed. He would confirm my contention that the Western Cooperage logging camp was the best and biggest in all creation, including the moon and Canada, where my cousins Bud and Dorothy Banks lived.

In its time the Western Cooperage was among the better camps in which to live but even though God seemed to agree with me in my daydreams that it was, it wasn't the biggest. The Kerry Line, out past Jewell, kept trainloads of logs moving out of its Camp Neverstill day and night. On their return trips from the log dump on the Columbia River below the town of Clatskanie the locomotives would often become virtual freight trains with box cars of supplies, machinery, and merchandise for Nehalem Valley farmers and residents of the dozen or more isolated logging camps scattered along the company railroad.

Camp Neverstill was almost like a city since it had a store and even a hospital. The fabulous Kerry Line has long since been a memory. The only reminder of its glorious past is a many-windowed structure that used to be a railroad round-house and machine shop. It sits in a farm field and is now doing duty as a barn and storage shed. At the log-dump end of the line on the Columbia River are the crumbling remains of rotted piling that once were log sorting areas and railroad trestles.

God had to make a few concessions in permitting me to visualize the Western Cooperage as the biggest of all camps but He was understanding of little boys and allowed me that special liberty.

Although God got along famously with Dad and Mother and me in these reveries He had problems with Uncle Marsh. Uncle Marsh was as big as Dad and ten times as stubborn. He was also impatient and quick-tempered. Whenever I'd manage to bring God and him together they'd go at it hot and heavy with Uncle Marsh ordering God around just as though He were people. It used to tickle me to picture God winking at Dad and taking orders from Uncle Marsh.

Sometimes, in these moments of daydreaming, I'd have Dad let Uncle Marsh in on the secret. He'd say something like, "Now hold up there a minute, Marsh. This is no ordinary logger you're bossing around. This is God."

Try as I might, even in my daydreams, I could never maneuver Uncle Marsh to a point where he was at a loss for words, or flustered, or even surprised. Standing there, face to face with God, he'd take the initiative. "When I git up there," he'd say, pointing overhead, "You give the orders. But when You're down here with my crew I give the orders. You remember that and You and me ain't likely to have any trouble."

On one occasion I got so carried away with my daydreaming that when Uncle Marsh and God got to arguing over something I burst into an audible giggle. Mother heard me and wanted to know what I was laughing about. I was mortified at having to confess I had been daydreaming. I told her about God and Uncle Marsh and how, in my daydreams, Uncle Marsh always seemed to get the better of it in their arguments.

"Don't you worry about God," she told me, "He can take care of Himself." She then pulled Dad's big rocking chair around so it faced me and my little rocker. She sat down and we had a little heart to heart talk. Imagination was a wonderful thing, she said, and was a special gift from God to man that enabled man to plan, think, and progress. Daydreaming was a little bit like imagination, she said, but she described it as imagination without action. All little boys with active minds daydreamed, she said, but she cautioned against letting daydreaming become a habit.

"When you daydream," she said, "put legs on your dreams and make them go someplace. A daydream with legs is imagination." Thomas Edison, she said, had imagination, as did Alexander Bell, who invented the telephone. So did Mr. Woodrow Wilson, the President of the United States.

"You can aim your imagination exactly as you aim your air rifle," she told me. I was too young to grasp her meaning fully but Mother operated on the theory that ideas were like seeds—you planted them early and with proper nourishment and care they were almost certain to take root and grow. One of her earliest gardening efforts with me was implanting the idea that I would one day go to college. The idea never fully germinated in my own mind but although my imagination in so far as an education was concerned was never firmly on target, Mother's was. When the time came I did go to college.

But getting back to God. He got along famously with our family and was accepted and respected by most of the other families and single men in the camp. But there were times when His presence created problems and complicated our lives.

One of those times was when a young couple, whom I'll call the Michelsons although that wasn't their real name, moved to the camp. Mrs. Michelson was vivacious, always smiling or laughing, and pretty as a picture. Her husband was a rather effeminate, quiet individual who never entered into any of the camp's meager social activities.

Mother described him as a taciturn man. Uncle Marsh referred to him as "that sour-faced sonofabitch." Dad passed him off as a fellow who wasn't much of a talker.

Everyone in camp liked Mrs. Michelson. Mother was the only one who went out of her way and made an effort to understand and be friendly with Mr. Michelson. She discovered that he was quite an authority on the Bible and was anxious to start a Sunday school in camp. Dad doubted that he'd have much success.

In the first place, said Dad, Mr. Michelson didn't have the confidence and respect of people in the camp. Secondly, the camp residents were friendly and considerate but they were furiously independent. Dad doubted that they would take kindly to someone like Mr. Michelson telling them their children ought to go to Sunday school.

"I'll help him," said Mother. "This camp needs a Sunday school."

As a sort of trial balloon to test camp acceptance of the idea, she contacted Mrs. Johnson. "We Johnsons got a Good Book stored in the family trunk and if we be aneedin' some lessoning I reckon Fen or Jake could read it to us," she told Mother. Fen and Jake were Mrs. Johnson's boys. They were five or six years older than I was and already expert hunters, trappers, and skilled users of tobacco and cuss words. Both boys thoroughly despised the wasted hours they had to spend on the three R's in our one-room school.

Mother knew that if she could get Mrs. Johnson to send Fen and Jake to the Sunday school it would have a good psychological reaction on the rest of the camp. No honest Christian could be so callous, she reasoned, as to stand idly by and see the Good Lord set upon by two such hell raisers as Fen and Jake. But talk wasn't going to sway Mrs. Johnson.

Mother had a hole card that she was keeping especially for Mrs. Johnson. She played it now.

In our bureau drawer at home was a bottle of good whiskey that Dad and Mother used for medicinal purposes. If Dad or I had a touch of sore throat we would get a sip of raw whiskey to kill the germs. A head cold called for a hot toddy —a little whiskey mixed with hot water and a bit of sugar as sweetener. Then into bed to relax and perspire and usually by morning the cold would be gone or definitely on the mend. Dad had been having a lot of throat trouble the past few months so the old bottle was exhausted and a brand new bottle, not yet opened, was in the drawer. Mother took it over to Mrs. Johnson's. She set it on the kitchen table and bluntly made her offer: the bottle of whiskey in return for Mrs. Johnson's promise that Fen and Jake would attend the Sunday school.

Mrs. Johnson contemplated the offer and puffed thoughtfully on her corncob pipe for a moment or two. "If the good Lord is that determined to have Fen and Jake in your school, I guess He shouldn't be denied," she finally agreed. Opening the bottle, she poured a healthy slug of the amber liquor for herself and a wee sip for Mother into two enamel cups. Lifting her cup to her lips, she sniffed the contents and then with a little gesture that was almost a curtsy said to Mother: "You say when, Caroline, and my boys will be there. I promise."

A few nights later Dad came home with a touch of sore throat. It seemed to disappear suddenly when Mother told him he'd have to gargle with salt water.

Mother's intuition had been correct. Word soon spread around the camp that Fen and Jake Johnson would be attending Sunday school classes when they started. Mr. Michelson was elated. In fact he was so happy he almost smiled. As Mrs. Johnson had promised to see that Fen and Jake attended, other parents said they'd be willing to enroll their youngsters.

"I'll never know how you did it," Mr. Michelson told Mother.

"The Lord works in quiet but victorious ways," said Mother.

"He does indeed," agreed Mr. Michelson. "In the army of the Lord there is no such word as defeat."

Mr. Michelson had no way of knowing that within a few months the camp would turn on him and he would suffer a cruel and humiliating defeat. Mother termed it a headstrong, barbarous eruption of animal hatreds and emotions. Dad said it was the Lord's way of testing Mr. Michelson's real sincerity and faith and that on both counts Mr. Michelson had failed.

But on the opening day of the Sunday school there was no hint of resentment among the parents. Most of them actually seemed relieved and pleased that the camp was really going to have a Sunday school. Mrs. Johnson did as she had promised Mother. A few minutes before the class was to start in the schoolhouse she came waddling down the graveled county road with a long willow switch in her right hand, herding Fen and Jake with the skill of farmer Dave Tweedle handling the pigs he kept penned at the camp to take advantage of free slop and waste food from the cookhouse.

Each time one of the boys seemed about to make a break for freedom Mrs. Johnson appeared to anticipate the intention. She'd reach out and lay the tip of the switch across the calf of a bare leg. The sting would set both boys to pleading. "Dammit, Ma, lay off that switch," or "Ma, for Pete's sake, I got welts from my ass to my ankles."

A few parents, Mother among them, sat in on the first classes to see what Mr. Michelson had in mind. Mrs. Johnson surprised everyone by staying too. Mr. Michelson, a little indignantly I thought, told her she was welcome but that when she was in the House of the Lord she would have to remove the corncob pipe from her mouth and keep it in her apron pocket.

For one tense, awful moment I thought she was going to march right up to Mr. Michelson and give him a face to face cuss-out that would bring bolts of lightning from Heaven down on the schoolhouse and us. Mother spoke up and kept an incident from erupting into a battle. She said that in her opinion Mr. Michelson was right; that the folks present, including the young people, should be able to do without a smoke or a chew of tobacco or snoose for the hour or so of Sunday school; she also pointed out that Mr. Michelson was giving up some of his free time each Sunday to teach us kids a little more about God and the Bible and parents especially should be grateful and co-operate. While she talked she riveted Mrs. Johnson to her seat with a glare that was as merciless and cold as the point of a diamond drill.

The Sunday school was moderately successful. I was a regular attender and so were Fen and Jake Johnson. The rest of the kids in camp came regularly at first and then their attendance became more and more irregular until some didn't come at all any more. Mr. Michelson was at fault. We all enjoyed the classes immensely when his wife taught. She was young and pretty and had a soft, musical voice that made listening and learning a pleasure. Also, she used the natural things around us—the forest, wildlife, summer skies, Klaskanine Creek, good people who lived in the camp—as examples of God's work.

Mr. Michelson stuck straight with the Bible. He would get angry if you so much as listened to a robin sing while he was talking. He didn't like it if we looked out the window. If we did something that displeased him during the regular session he'd keep us after class and read us long passages from the Bible as atonement and punishment.

He frightened us with talk that the other boys and girls in camp who didn't attend Sunday school were doomed for Hell and that the rest of us weren't saved by a long shot just because we were there each Sunday. He implanted fear and uneasiness rather than trust and comfort. Mrs. Johnson was the first to voice openly the discontent felt by others in the camp at the methods Mr. Michelson employed. Since she had

made a promise of sorts to Mother she took her complaint
to her.

"That man is scarin' hell out of my Fen and Jake," she
told Mother. "He talks like a man from the Devil." On the
basis of some of the things I had mentioned Mother and Dad
weren't too happy with Mr. Michelson, either. Dad agreed
with Mrs. Johnson that it was about time for someone to
take a hand and set Mr. Michelson straight on a few things.
For one, the parents in the camp had perhaps unconsciously
taught their children to accept God as one of them and part
of the camp community, not to live in fear and awe of Him.

Mother, because she had been active in supporting Mr.
Michelson and helping get the Sunday school started, felt
responsible for whatever might happen, good or bad. She dis-
liked Mr. Michelson's tactics but felt he was doing in his own
way what he sincerely believed was best for us kids and for
the spiritual betterment of the entire camp. A Sunday school
of any sort was better than no Sunday school, she argued.
An uneasy truce prevailed for a while longer but finally the
camp came to a decision. Mother was chosen to succeed Mr.
Michelson as Sunday school teacher. It would also be her
responsibility to tell him of the change.

Mother was able to arrange a compromise. Mr. Michelson
would be permitted to go on teaching if he'd cut out the
Hell fire and brimstone. If he wouldn't agree to that then
maybe he'd agree to letting his wife do the teaching instead
of him. The suggestion was agreeable to the other parents in
camp. There was only one hitch—Mr. Michelson gave
Mother a flat "no" when she told him what the camp
wanted. The Sunday school was his idea, he said; he'd gotten
his inspiration from God, God helped him get it started, and
God wanted him, Mr. Michelson, to do the teaching.

Mother cautiously pointed out that it was she, not Mr.
Michelson, who had gotten most of the parents to agree to
send their youngsters to the Sunday school. She also told him
that a majority of the parents in the camp didn't feel that his

7. This is how some of the neighbors lived when Big Sam brought his bride from Boston to the logging camp.

8. Western Cooperage Company's headquarters camp as it appeared in 1921. The Churchill house is the one at the far left with the large shed attached. The small house next to it on the right was provided for the schoolteacher.

9. Young Sam, at the right, in the one-room school.

10. The author and a friend, perched on a large stump, survey the results of the loggers' work. This was when there was still plenty of timber left.

11. A hot day at the headquarters camp in 1917. Young Sam stands where the logging railroad crossed the county road.

12. Looking down the logging railroad that ran in front of the Churchill home. Caroline Churchill's sweet-pea bed is at the left of the tracks.

13. A Shay locomotive formerly owned by Western Cooperage. Young Sam and his mother rode in the cab of this little fellow many a time.

14. Camp Two—where Young Sam's mother brought him to pick wild blackberries. Bunkhouses for the men are in the rear, the cookhouse in the foreground. *(Photo courtesy of Ball Studio, Astoria, Oregon)*

15. A timber faller stands on the springboard from which he and a partner placed the undercut in this big Douglas fir. In the early days trees were cut as much as ten feet above ground to avoid the swell at the base.

way of teaching was necessarily God's way, that the parents wanted their children to love God, not fear Him.

Mr. Michelson told Mother she was a disciple of the Devil and ordered her out of his house. Mother never breathed a word to anyone, except Dad, what had really taken place when she talked with Mr. Michelson. But Mr. Michelson was less secretive. He seemed to relish retelling exactly what had happened. He said Mother was a messenger from Hell, that she came to him with words from the Devil, and that he had demanded she clear out of his house.

Dad's patience was as absorbent as an overgrown sponge but the limits of his patience and pride were finally reached. After being informed of a particularly bitter tirade by Mr. Michelson against Mother, Dad began whittling a heavy cedar shake into what appeared to be a paddle.

Mother thought he was going to use it on me. I was a little apprehensive myself although at the moment I couldn't for the life of me think of any wrong I had done that Dad could possibly know about.

"This isn't for Samuel," Dad replied in answer to obvious looks of anxiety from both Mother and myself.

"Then who is it for?" Mother wanted to know.

"For that spoiled fathead Michelson," said Dad. With clenched jaw and jutting chin he whittled away at the heavy shake and told Mother his plan. He was going to drape Mr. Michelson across his knees and apply the shake paddle where it would do the most good. "It's something his own father should have done thirty years ago," said Dad. Mother was horrified. She never before had seen Big Sam so riled up with anger. Outwardly, except for the knotted muscles along his jaw line and the flash of the pocketknife blade as it bit into the soft wood of the cedar shake, Dad appeared calm. But inside he seethed with what was near to homicidal rage. In his present mood and with his bull-like strength and the thick cedar paddle he could easily mangle every blood vessel in poor Mr. Michelson's fat-cheeked behind.

Mother pleaded and argued, to no avail. Dad just kept on whittling. "You're not doing this for me," she finally declared. "You're doing it solely for your own silly pride." Dad merely grunted. "I've never seen you this way before," Mother persisted.

"I've never been this mad before," Dad reminded her.

"If you insist on being mad at somebody or something why not get mad at that wood log," Mother suggested, pointing to a big fir log that, once sawed and split into stovewood size, would be our winter wood supply. The company sold its waste logs to employees for five dollars each, delivered by railroad car to your front yard.

The sight of the wood log gave Mother an idea. "Before you spank Mr. Michelson will you do one thing for me?" she asked. Before committing himself Dad wanted to know what it was she wanted done. "It's nothing unreasonable," she assured him. The paddle was almost ready for use. "A wife should be entitled to one last favor before her husband is carted off to jail," Mother insisted. She kept needling and the knife blade kept flashing along the cedar shake faster and faster as Dad became angrier and angrier.

"All right," he finally stormed in exasperation, "tell me what you want done and I'll do it."

"Saw a block off the wood log before you go," said Mother. The length of log had to be sawed into blocks of stovewood length. It was bone-hard muscle work with a crosscut saw. The big blocks could then be quartered like a pie with a sledge hammer and wedges and the smaller chunks then split into stove and kindling wood with an ax.

Mother's request seemed utterly ridiculous to Dad. It seemed equally pointless to me. Why worry about a wood log when Dad was about to kill a man? "Carrie," said Dad, "sometimes you just don't make good sense."

"And neither do you," Mother snapped back. Since he had promised to do Mother's bidding Dad pocketed his knife,

laid the shake paddle carefully on the wood log, and grum-
bling, went to the woodshed and got the crosscut saw.

The wood log was a fairly hefty one, about four feet in
diameter. Dad had been sawing about fifteen minutes and
the sweat was beginning to pop from his forehead and temples
and trickle down his cheeks when he suddenly stopped sawing. Breathing heavily from the physical exertion, he turned
to Mother and with a look of purest admiration and respect
garnished with one of his most boyish smiles told her: "The
luckiest day of my life was when I married you."

"It was my luckiest too," said Mother, dabbing at her eyes
with a corner of her apron and hurrying toward the house.

I started to follow but Dad called me back. "You stay out
here awhile and chop some kindling," he said, tousling my
hair, "I want to talk with your mother—alone."

"Then will you whip Mr. Michelson?" I asked eagerly.

"No," he said slowly. "I guess I'll never whip Mr. Michelson now. That wood log and saw took all the fight out of
me."

I couldn't understand how a wood log and a crosscut saw
could have anything to do with Dad not spanking Mr. Michelson. But then, grown-ups were sometimes difficult to understand. Mother later tried to explain it to me. Sometimes, she
said, when you get so mad you want to hit someone, if you
stop and count to ten, or run up to the machine shop and
back you'd forget all about being mad and wouldn't want
to fight any more.

She said that was what Mr. Michelson was trying to teach
us at Sunday school and all of us could help him by doing
our best to be understanding and patient.

Although Dad and Mother adopted an attitude of understanding and patience toward Mr. Michelson the rest of the
camp didn't. Mother and Dad were not included in a final
decision by which a group of camp residents decided the
Michelsons must go. It resulted in a sordid display of mob
rule rare in logging camp ethics. Mother was heartsick, Dad

was disgusted, and I was shocked and terrified that people I loved and admired could be so mean.

It all started shortly after Dad's near bout with Mr. Michelson. Someone, half jokingly, suggested that since Mr. Michelson wouldn't relinquish his Sunday school teaching post to anyone else and had taken on such high and mighty airs recently, it might be well to show him once and for all who was boss. Maybe toss a few rotten eggs at his house; dunk him in the frigid waters of Klaskanine Creek; watch him go into his outhouse some night, then wrap and padlock a length or two of chain around the tiny structure so he couldn't open the door and leave him locked up inside.

Finally it was suggested that maybe the camp had put up with him long enough. Why not bombard his house with rotten eggs, cookhouse slop, rotted vegetables, and pigpen dung. Drive him right out of camp. The problem of his wife was brought up. It was decided that though everyone liked her, if she chose to live with the likes of a Mr. Michelson then she'd have to share the abuse and humiliation. It was regrettable but it was one of the facts of married life, the same as being married to a drunk or a thief.

Mother and Dad knew something was up, but they didn't know what. Dad came across a cache of rotten eggs, old vegetables, and other stuff in the woods one day. He wondered at the time if somebody was hiding them for a purpose. Mother pooh-poohed his suspicion. No one in the Western Cooperage camp would be that crude, she argued.

But one night, shortly after dark, there was more than the normal amount of foot traffic up and down the railroad track that went by our house. There were snickers and giggles and muffled conversations. I recognized the voices of some of my playmates. Suddenly the quiet of the night erupted into a welter of shouts and jeers and catcalls. A friend of mine banged on our kitchen door. When Mother opened it he stood in the faint glow of lamplight with eyes glistening. He was so beside himself with excitement he could barely make himself understood. He finally calmed down sufficiently to report that they were rotten-egging the Michelsons out of camp and to hurry up or we would miss all the fun.

Mother was too astonished to do anything but stare at him for a moment or two before telling him to run along. She closed the door and with her back against it looked as though she were about to faint. Dad grabbed her and eased her into a chair.

"Those poor, dear people," she kept murmuring over and over to herself. "What can we do?"

Nothing, Dad told her. This was Mr. Michelson's affair. He'd have to handle it himself. Dad's attitude galvanized Mother into action. Adrenalin must have been pouring into her system by the quart.

"What do you mean, nothing?" she almost screamed at Dad. "Do you mean you'd sit here placidly and unconcerned while a bunch of heathen bastards drive two fine people from their home?" Mother's use of the term "bastards" was more of a shock to Dad than what was going on down at the Michelsons'. He just stared at her with mouth agape. By the time he recovered Mother had slammed the door open and was half-way out into the darkness. "Sit here and be damned," she shouted back over her shoulder. "I'll be down with Mr. and Mrs. Michelson."

I made a jump toward the door to follow, but Dad grabbed me by a shoulder. His fingers dug in with the hurt of steel. I cried out in surprise and pain. He relaxed his grip with a mumbled "I'm sorry." He motioned toward the cot that was my bed in the corner of the room. "You sit," he ordered. I could hear the hoots and jeers of the crowd as it tossed eggs and vegetables. I could hear Mother yelling, "Stop this. Do you hear me? Stop this right now."

In our small, one-room house there wasn't much room to pace. But Dad made the most of what there was. He swung back and forth between the kitchen door at one end and the wood-burning heating stove at the other. Sometimes he strode with the smooth easy grace of a panther. At other times he reminded me of a lumbering, full-grown black bear. Every now and then as he swung back and forth within the restricted confines I'd hear him mutter to himself, "Women! Damn silly women."

The howls and jeers of the egg-throwing crowd at the Michelsons' grew louder. There was a change in the timbre of the voices. It was something you sensed rather than heard. There was less laughter and a more brittle tone to the cat-calls and shouts. Dad stopped his pacing and listened intently for a moment, as though measuring the shift of the crowd's mood.

Suddenly we both heard Mother call. Her voice sounded small and terribly frightened. "Sam! Sam!" she was pleading, "come quickly." Dad turned to me. He reached out one of his big hands and patted my head. "You stay right here," he said. Then he whirled and leaped for the open kitchen door. As he lunged through the opening one shoulder sideswiped the door frame. The house shuddered from the impact.

I listened as his long strides swept him down the railroad track. I heard him yelling at the crowd. I knew it was Dad but it wasn't his voice. It was wild and shrill like the hunting call of the stalking cougar that sometimes lurked around the camp and gave out with its weird, lonely cry in the middle of the night.

I rolled over on my belly, buried my head in a pillow, and began to sob.

Above the sound of my own sobbing I could hear Dad's shouts and orders. There were other voices. They reflected inner irritations, angers, and confusion. "Take your wife and git on home, Sam." "We don't want no trouble with you, Sam." "This is between Michelson and us, Sam."

And then, suddenly, above the welter of noise came the annoyed, gravelly bellow of Mrs. Johnson. "Will someone tell me what in the name of hell is going on here? Can't a body get a night's sleep in this God damn camp no more?"

Mrs. Johnson's inquiry startled the crowd into almost absolute silence. In the half-light from a star-filled sky she apparently saw the egg and rotten-vegetable splotches. I could only guess but there was no doubt about how she felt when she again spoke. I doubt that any group of loggers, and their wives, have been so soundly and roundly cursed at any time before or since.

She ended her tirade with the dire promise that "If I was God by all that's holy I'd run the lot of you bare-assed through a briar patch."

There was some self-conscious and muffled laughter and then the sounds of a crowd breaking up. Feet began shuffling up the railroad track past our house as their owners headed away from the Michelsons' and toward their own homes.

Mother and Dad brought the Sunday school teacher and his wife to our house. The woman was hysterical and crying. Mother had an arm around her and was trying to comfort her. Now that the danger was passed Mr. Michelson was indignant and no longer cowering or frightened. "Beasts. That's what they are, beasts. I'll have the law on them," he kept saying, wagging a finger at Dad as though in some way he were responsible for what had happened. "You mark my words, Mr. Sam Churchill. If necessary I'll see to it this whole filthy camp is locked up."

Dad reached out and with a hand under each of Mr. Michelson's armpits lifted him clear of the floor and high enough so he could look him square in the face. "You'll be doing me a favor," he said, "if you'll just shut your dirty little mouth for a while and try comforting your wife." He was still holding Mr. Michelson in the air when Mrs. Johnson appeared at the open kitchen door. In her hand was the bottle of whiskey Mother had given her to assure Fen and Jake's attendance at Sunday school.

"Somebody left the cork off this so there ain't much left," she apologized to Mother, "but they's enough to give the little woman there a lift." She nodded toward Mrs. Michelson.

Dad had set Mr. Michelson back down on the floor. He swung toward Mrs. Johnson and pushed the bottle aside, almost knocking it from her hand in the process. "We don't use liquor," he said sternly. Looking as angelic as it was possible for her to look, and without a trace of animosity in her voice, Mrs. Johnson took hold of Mr. Michelson's shirt front, drew him close, and almost whispered: "This is for your wife. As for you I wouldn't give you a bottle of cold piss."

Logging camp people find it impossible to hold a grudge or nurse an anger. It wasn't long before some of those who had been in on the rotten-egging were poking their heads in the kitchen door, which was still open, and with sheepish looks and shrugs trying to tell Mother and Dad in their own way that they were sorry for what had happened. When they saw the Michelsons they apologized to them, too.

Some of the wives then hurried home only to return in a few minutes with cakes, cookies, and whatever else was handy in their own kitchens. Dad tossed some pitchy wood, kindling, and a little kerosene in the kitchen stove and in less time than it would take Mrs. Johnson to say "everybody drink up" had a roaring fire going. Mother put a kettle of water on the stove and in no time at all there was a boiling pot of coffee.

The horrible incident of little more than an hour ago had suddenly turned into a noisy, chattery, carefree party.

The party did not mean that the people in camp had changed their minds and decided that the Michelsons should stay. They had decreed that Mr. Michelson had to go. That decision still held. The party was merely an expression of regret for the manner in which the camp people had behaved.

Early the next morning Mr. Michelson and his wife loaded the few household possessions they owned into a borrowed old Model T truck. Mother and a few other wives were there to express their regrets and wish them well. Mrs. Johnson was there too. And so was I. "I wish you wouldn't go," I said to Mrs. Michelson. She removed my cap and kissed the top of my head. "You are a fine boy, Samuel," she said. "Someday you'll grow into a big, strong man like your father."

Turning to Mrs. Johnson, she took her hand and squeezing it until her own knuckles turned white said: "God bless you, Mrs. Johnson. I know He is keeping a special place for you in His heart."

That night at supper Dad asked Mother a question that had been bothering him all day at work. "How," he wanted to know, "did Mrs. Johnson get my bottle of whiskey?"

## Chapter 8

### FEN JOHNSON

It was a warm spring morning and Mother was outside hanging up the family wash when she happened to notice Fen Johnson ambling up the railroad track past our house. In one hand he had an alder pole and in the other a can of worms.

"Fen Johnson," Mother called from between the flapping rows of work clothes, drop-seat underwear, and other logging camp apparel, "why aren't you in school?" Fen quickened his pace but didn't answer.

To me, not yet of school age and busy laying out a miniature logging operation along the ridge of a low dirt bank near the clotheslines, the answer was obvious: Fen was going fishing.

As a matter of fact it wasn't at all unusual for Fen to skip school and go fishing. Frankly, it wasn't unusual for half the one-room school's enrollment of eight pupils to sneak out on warm spring days and go fishing.

This indifference to the responsibilities of acquiring an education was unacceptable to Mother. Standing at the clothesline with a couple of clothespins clamped between her teeth watching Fen continue up the railroad track, Mother decided it was time for action.

Dropping the pins in the pockets of the clothespin bag tied like an apron around her waist, Mother cleared my miniature logging project and a drainage ditch alongside the railroad track in one long leap. Her feet landed on the ties between the rails at full throttle and before Fen had a chance to leap to safety in the underbrush Mother had him by a handful of hair and he was fanning the air with his toes like an acrobatic dancer.

"It's time we had a talk with your mother," Mother was declaring grimly as she swung him in a tight circle and headed him down a narrow path through the brush toward his house.

Alerted by Fen's yowling, prompted by fear and imagined pain, Mrs. Johnson was waiting as Mother and Fen, with me following, burst from the mouth of the path that emptied into the little clearing surrounding the Johnson house.

She wasn't a particularly reassuring sight. A plump, rather squat woman, she stood with feet apart and in house slippers. In her hand was a broom, the original handle of which had been replaced with a heavy piece of alder limb. In her mouth was her corncob pipe. Little dribbles of smoke trickled from her mouth as she watched the three of us approach. Now and then a stream of smoke would tumble from one nostril after being expelled the long way around through one clear sinus and nasal passage.

Mother planted Fen, whimpering, firmly in front of his own mother. "Mrs. Johnson," she said brushing a whiff of smoke from Mrs. Johnson's pipe away from her face, "Fen's been playing hookey from school."

"God A'mighty, Caroline," exclaimed Mrs. Johnson with a sigh that was a mixture of irritation and relief, "the way you come tearin' through the brush with him I thought he'd kilt somebody."

Only himself, said Mother, wagging a finger under Mrs. Johnson's nose. She went on to explain that every day of school Fen missed was a day of lost opportunity that would never again be his. "Do you want Fen to grow up to be an intellectual corpse?" asked Mother.

"A corpse," exploded Mrs. Johnson. "He eats like a pig and he's healthy as a horse." She added that his grandparents on both sides lived into their nineties and Fen would likely do the same.

She was also of the opinion that young fellows like Fen and his brother Jake had just so much room for learning. Both boys could already read and write, she argued, and you go pushing them too much and they might end up sick. She also, with admirable restraint and patience, explained to Mother that the human brain was like a bucket. It held so much and beyond that you could feed it education until hell froze over and never gain a thing. The excess would simply spill over and drain away. It made sense to me and I could almost see stuff Fen's brain couldn't take running out his ears and nose.

Fen was beginning to feel a lot better. "My ma can whip your ma," he half-snarled at me, turning at the same time to poke out his tongue at Mother. Mrs. Johnson brought the heavy alder handle of the broom across his behind with a jolt that almost bowled him over.

"By Jesus," she roared, "if they's one thing the old man and me won't put up with it's a young'un with no manners." Laying on another clout, she ordered Fen to "Git your hinder back to school and you stay there until you learn manners." She finished up with a dire warning that "Any more hookey business and I'll blister you good."

"Fen is assured of at least an eighth grade education," Mother smilingly predicted to Dad that night at supper.

Fen was a gangling lad not yet in his teens who knew as many cuss words as most grown-up loggers. He rolled me my first cigarette and gave me my first chew of tobacco, each of which made me deathly sick. In summer it was he who knew where the wild blackberries were thickest and biggest. And he knew almost to the day when the luscious blue huckleberries would be full ripe and sweetest.

He knew every creek, canyon and woodland trail for miles around and had a sense of direction as unerring as a compass. He was a dead shot with his .22 caliber rifle, a prized possession he often brought to school and stored upright in a corner near his desk during classes.

All of us youngsters in camp had hopes and dreams for the future. Most wanted to take up a line of work similar to that of their fathers. Fen was one of the exceptions. Merton and Wilbur Cox wanted to be locomotive engineers the same as their dad. Rex Gaynor, my age and my closest friend, had hopes of becoming a timber cruiser, as was his father. Timber cruisers surveyed timber properties, estimated the probable quantity per acre, and sometimes would be back in the hills for weeks at a time locating property lines and recording other information.

Phil Peets aimed to be a donkey engine operator. Oddly, none of us as I recall had any desire to work in the office or be foremen or civil engineers or machinists or any of the many highly skilled jobs available that paid high salaries. High, at least, in comparison with the day-worker jobs connected directly with the bone-hard work of getting the logs from tree stump to railroad loading site.

The probable reason was that our fathers for the most part were not in the executive group. They were heavy-muscled men who fought mud, heat, cold, and wet and a prohibitive terrain gouged, slashed, and heaped into massive disorder by nature. Demanding and cruel as it was at times, it was a fascinating land and we young people loved it and wanted always to be part of it.

Fen loved it too, but in a way different from the rest of us. The crashing thunder of falling trees, the throaty voice of the big machines, the shouts and curses of sweating, straining men never seemed to excite Fen as they excited us.

He could sit by the hour alongside a crystal pool of Klaskanine Creek watching a half-dozen trout idling against the current. I've watched him sit motionless on a stump while a family of deer, unaware of his presence, browsed within a few feet of him. Born and reared in the heavy rainfall area of the Oregon Coast Range mountains we automatically learned to accept and appreciate rain. It was, we knew, the abundance of rain that produced the magnificent forest that was our home and the provider of jobs for our fathers and probable careers for us in later years.

Fen loved rain. I remember one overcast summer day he and I hiked several miles down the railroad to a special fishing hole Fen had discovered. While we were there a fleet of thunderheads rolled in and suddenly we were in the midst of a wild outburst of rain, wind, thunder, and lightning. I cowered in panic under a low trestle where the railroad crossed a small gully. It was no protection from the wind and rain but it was a shield from falling trees, and there were many crashing to earth around us.

I pleaded with Fen to join me; not so much for his protection but as a companion to share the misery of my own fear. He tried to shame me out of my timidity but I was frightened beyond being shamed and not about to venture from the protective timbers of the trestle. Meanwhile Fen stripped off his clothes, which consisted of shirt, pants, and shoes, and pranced back and forth across the trestle in mock defiance of nature. He screeched and howled in pure delight as the needle points of rain bit into the bare white nakedness of his body.

The storm passed as suddenly as it came. I emerged from under the trestle shivering-cold and soaking wet. Fen retrieved his clothes, snug and dry, from under a log where he had deposited them. Shaking himself like a dog that has just finished a swim, he slipped back into his clothes and we headed up the railroad track toward camp and home . . . Fen, buoyant, fresh, and exuberant; me, cold, soggy, and miserable.

On the way home we talked. Fen couldn't understand my fear of storms. I couldn't explain it either except that the bigness of nature sometimes scared me.

"Things you like won't hurt you," said Fen. He said he liked bees, had never stolen honey from a bee tree, and could go right up to the hole in the tree and watch the bees going in and out without getting stung.

He said he had picked blackberries at one end of a patch while a bear greedily gobbled his share at the opposite end. He also confided that he had seen the cougar that sometimes stalked the camp on winter nights and set all the dogs to howling. "He wouldn't hurt anybody," declared Fen, "he's old and lonely."

One night, months later, with snow a foot deep and the camp wrapped in the cocoon of winter, hysterical barking of the camp dogs jolted me from a sound sleep. Goose pimples crawled along the surface of my skin in ripples of alarm and uneasiness. Something leaped out of the darkness onto the cot that was my bed and I went rigid with terror until I discovered it was our cat, Muff, a half-wild mistress who shunned human interference at birthing time and had her kittens in an abandoned burrow under a stump.

She thumped across the bedcovers stiff-legged and crouched on the pillow beside my head. I reached out and touched her and found her fur bristled and almost as stiff as splinters. Moments later she was on her feet, back arched and tail stiff as a ramrod. And then I heard it; the half-human scream of the cougar. It seemed to come from the timbered slope across the railroad from our house and up behind Rex Gaynor's. I could almost visualize the hungry beast clawing away the shingle shakes from Rex Gaynor's house.

Remembering what Fen had told me about the cougar being old and lonely I tried to picture it as a jolly old animal version of Daddy Hoyt with laughing gray eyes, white beard, and white hair. Daddy Hoyt was the "stationary" engineer in charge of the boiler and steam engine that powered equipment in the machine shop. But try as I might the cougar maintained its blood-chilling image of blazing yellow-green eyes and gleaming white fangs. Rocketing from the cot, I piled under the covers between Dad and Mother in the lean-to bedroom. Seconds later Muff came scampering in.

Mother, her maternal instinct at work even though she was half asleep, tucked the covers firmly under my chin. Dad, flat on his back with mouth partly open, snored peacefully on while, to my mind, Rex and the entire Gaynor family were being eaten alive by the cougar.

Next morning I asked Fen if he had heard the cougar. He'd not only heard it, he said, he'd gotten dressed and by lantern light went almost up to Rex Gaynor's in hopes he might see it. It was cold and the fresh fallen snow was hard to walk in so he'd given up and returned home.

I'd never actually known Fen to lie about anything but I was certain he was lying now and I told him so. His honor at stake, he took me to the old railroad grade that passed by the front of Gaynors' house. There was no doubting Fen's word any longer. There in the fresh fall of snow were his tracks along with some frozen brown splotches of tobacco juice. He'd walked only a little way up the old grade before turning around, just as he said. So that there would be no lingering doubts in my mind he removed one of his shoes and set it in one of the shoe tracks. It fitted the indentation perfectly.

While kneeling down in the snow fitting the shoe into the track, we noticed something that neither of us had been aware of previously. On his return Fen had had company. The evidence was the roundish pug marks of an animal. They were as big as the palm of Big Sam's hand.

"Them's not dog tracks," Fen assured me, lacing up his shoe. "Them's cat tracks. That old cougar devil was follering me."

I wanted to tell everyone in camp about Fen being outdoors all alone in the middle of the night and a hungry cougar following him but he made me promise to never tell a soul.

"If Ma knowed I sneaked out of the house at night she'd wale hell out of me," he pleaded.

Outside of his own family and my mother Fen didn't have

any real close friends in camp. Mother was drawn to him, I suspect, because of his love and understanding of nature.

"Fen may have faults but who doesn't?" she used to challenge Dad.

Dad could never muster up much sympathy for anyone with time to spend sitting on a stump watching deer browse, or climbing an alder tree to peer into a bird's nest, or watching trout in a creek pool, or lying on his back the afternoon long with fingers laced to form a rough pillow and watching clouds, a circling hawk and other inhabitants of a summer sky.

"But he's only a boy," Mother used to argue.

"He's a lazy, unmannered snip who wanders off fishing and lets his mother chop kindling," Dad would snort.

No matter what Dad and many of the others in camp thought of Fen and his rapport with nature, Mother had her own opinion. There were certain basic physical characteristics that were mirrors of an individual's heart, mind, and soul, Mother always contended. A man or woman with close-set eyes was likely to be selfish, egotistical, and a shallow thinker, Mother maintained. Thick lips combined with a loose jowl and narrow forehead indicated a person with base instincts and low mentality. She abhorred persons with shifty eyes and a limp handshake.

Fen, somehow, passed Mother's stern physical appearance test. "He's a boy with unusual charm and ability," she concluded. All Fen needed, she was certain, was a push to arouse his interest and get him in motion.

At times Fen sparked to life with enthusiasm and a real show of acceleration but usually not in quite the way Mother had in mind. There was the time he and his brother Jake got into the camp powder house where dynamite used in the logging and railroad construction operations was stored. They lugged off a couple of armloads of the stuff and set it off in Klaskanine Creek.

The resulting blast showered the camp with dead fish,

rock, water, and chunks of wood. Unfortunately the incident occurred during the height of I.W.W. (Industrial Workers of the World) strikes and disorders and virtually everyone in camp at first thought the Wobblies (the nickname given members of the group) were dynamiting the camp.

When T. W. Robinson, camp superintendent and a normally moderate, friendly man, found out what had really happened he and everybody else in camp except Mother and Mr. and Mrs. Johnson were ready to "accelerate" Fen right out of the county.

"I'll hang him head down from a tree and bust every bone in his body," raged T.W., and he was furious enough to do as he said. Mother intervened in Fen's behalf, and he got off with a strapping from his dad that left blue welts on his sitdown for more than a week. Jake got a good tongue-lashing and cussing but was spared further punishment because he was several years younger than Fen and the camp assumed he had been under the evil spell of his brother.

Following the dynamite incident, Mother had difficulty recruiting sympathizers and volunteers for her "Everybody Help Fen" fan club. Even Mrs. Johnson, his own mother, threw up her hands in defeat and despair.

"We done our best," she said wearily to Mother, "but the devil's got him. Believe me, Caroline, the devil's got him."

Despite an unusual number of awkward and annoying setbacks Fen did, on occasion, show promise under Mother's watchful eye. The year she put on a Christmas pageant in the camp cookhouse dining room Fen stole the show. He was one of the Wise Men. It was mostly pantomime but Fen succeeded in livening things up with a few "Gods" and "Jesuses," that definitely were not in the script. Bud Peets, an older boy, was David as I recall. He nearly put the audience into hysterics when in a fit of temper he snapped at Fen in a stage whisper that could be heard back to the last row of benches: "Dammit, Fen, look alive."

"I'll bet the Good Lord's doing some thinking," Dad chuckled at Mother.

"At least He knows we were trying," Mother shot back.

Fen's public image had horns and a forked tail after the dynamite incident but Mother's play did a lot toward restoring him to the good graces of the camp. It was an unexpected by-product that came about wholly by accident.

It happened this way: cases of canned goods from the cookhouse storeroom were stacked side by side and three high to form a stage. The cases were of various sizes so there were several step-ups and step-downs that the actors were supposed to avoid as they walked about the stage. Fen missed one of the step-ups near the scheduled end of the play, stumbled and pitched headfirst over the side of the stage to the cookhouse floor. He wasn't hurt, but the audience, seated on benches and tables, staggered as though drunk, intoxicated with unstoppable gales of laughter. There was no use trying to finish out the playlet and Mother let it die a natural but hilarious death. Old Mr. Johnson, Fen's dad, laughed so hard he splattered tobacco juice over the back of Five-Fingered Frenchy (George Paris), a railroad brakeman who had lost his fingers to link-and-pin couplings on logging railroad cars.

At any other time Frenchy would have stormed out of his seat swinging but he was doubled over with laugh cramps and spraying people in front of him. A fair quantity of tobacco juice that had been building up in a half-hundred mouths earlier in the evening shot to freedom as logger husbands and some of the older boys were caught off guard by Fen's unscheduled tumble. Dad and Uncle Marsh were among the guilty. Mrs. Johnson had great dribbles of juice clinging to her chin.

And in the overpowering excitement I wet my pants. A trickle skittered along the top of the bench and settled under the ample behind of Daddy Hoyt. As it began to soak through the seat of his bib overalls he roared to his feet with a terrible oath and began brushing the seat of his pants as though they were on fire. Everyone aimed his gaze at the new commotion and began pointing at the untidy wet stain. Even Mother didn't realize I was the guilty one. She was certain that Daddy Hoyt, limp and exhausted from laughing at Fen's mishap, had added a final comedy touch by wetting his pants.

It was another fifteen minutes before folks settled down enough to file outside, wipe the tears from their eyes, shake hands with Mother, and say good night. It was past bedtime before the camp settled down to its customary eight hours of sleep and quiet. Even then, at intervals, giggles and bursts of laughter would erupt from darkened houses.

Fen's improved public image following the play gave Mother new heart and determination in his behalf. "God gave each of us a talent," she used to insist.

"Then let God and Mrs. Johnson worry about Fen," was Dad's stock answer.

Much of Dad and Mother's household debate sessions about Fen was good-natured banter in which some of our closer friends in camp shared opinions. But when it came to real serious discussion about Fen's worth, Mother stood alone.

"I'd as soon mother a porcupine," said Mel Tate. Mr. Tate was a locomotive engineer on the Western Cooperage main line. He had been extremely critical of Fen and Jake since last Halloween, when his new, two-holer, family-type outhouse had been pushed over. He was certain Fen and Jake had done the pushing.

"Those without fault can cast the first stone," Mother would answer, putting in her own words a sentence from the Bible. This usually quieted Mr. Tate since it referred to the time she caught him cheating at cribbage. Mother had learned a few things about cards on Grandpa Snow's tugboat. She was so smooth at outcheating Mr. Tate at cheating that he finally complained to Dad. "Caroline's not cheating fair," he told Dad.

"Maybe they cheat differently in Boston," said Dad.

Mr. Tate said it was unladylike for a woman to cheat and he was of a mind not to play cribbage with Mother any more.

Mother and Mr. Tate finally agreed to a truce but they were so intent on watching each other that there was no longer any real pleasure in their cribbage games. Dad and Mrs. Tate finally persuaded them to quit playing cribbage.

"You are letting a silly card game spoil a good friendship," said Mrs. Tate.

"And I'm tired of playing cards with a crybaby," snipped Mother.

"And as of right now you've said enough," thundered Dad. And that ended the card playing.

But Mother continued her "Everybody Help Fen" project undismayed by the shrugs and doubts of the rest of the camp. Had she been permitted to continue the project the brush-covered site of the old Western Cooperage camp might be revered at this moment as the birthplace of Fen Johnson, internationally known surgeon, lawyer, or philosopher, or nature writer.

But she was denied the opportunity of finally proving her theory of Fen's untapped, inborn talent, whatever it might have been. Closure of the Western Cooperage school at the end of my fourth grade year forced Mother and Dad to live apart so that I could continue school. Mother and I moved to Seaside, a beach resort town twenty miles south of Astoria on the Oregon coast. Dad remained at the camp and came home weekends.

Mother never again saw Fen. It was several years after we had moved that I saw him once more. He was driving a rattly Model T Ford touring car without a top and had a few drinks too many. I was standing in front of Mr. Welker's store which had been built where the railroad crossed the county road. The store was a new venture at the camp since we had moved.

The old car pulled up abreast of the store. Without bothering to put it into neutral gear Fen turned off the ignition and let it buck to a halt. I walked over toward him as he continued to sit, half slouched, over the steering wheel.

"Hello Fen," I said. "I'm Sam Churchill." He turned and faced me and there was a flicker of recognition in his drink-dulled eyes.

"Well, if it ain't little Sam'l," he said. "How's your mother?" Years and liquor had taken a terrible physical and mental toll of Fen but they hadn't impaired the little memory corner that somehow he had reserved for Mother.

Later, when I reported seeing Fen, she was silent for a long moment. "God does give every man a talent," she said sadly. "With a little more time and patience I might have found Fen's. Was it God's will or my own ineptness that I didn't?"

I couldn't answer. I was thinking of that day so long ago when Fen, carefree and unfettered, went tramping up the railroad track past our house, obviously headed for a day of fishing. Maybe Fen just wasn't destined to be a big man, in terms of money and accomplishment.

On a recent visit to the old camp site I walked alongside Klaskanine Creek following a forest road that when I was a boy had been the Western Cooperage railroad track. It suddenly occurred to me that Fen Johnson had played a major role in shaping my life. He had taught me much about nature—that it wasn't a waste of time to observe and enjoy and try to interpret her moods and fancies.

The old camp area will always be Fen's country, but he shared many of its secrets with me, and that makes it my country too.

## Chapter 9

## SCHOOLHOUSE IN THE ROUGH

Education in the Western Cooperage school was informal but adequate, at least for the times. On pleasant spring days we were often permitted to spend a portion of the school day studying and reciting out of doors.

The school building, an unpainted, weather-polished, one-room structure with a home-cut cedar shake roof was mounted on log skids as was most every building in camp with the exception of the office, cookhouse, and machine shop. It was probably twelve to fifteen feet in width and possibly twenty or twenty-two feet long.

By today's standards it would have been subsubstandard in every respect, except in classroom load. One teacher taught all eight grades but enrollment averaged between six and ten pupils and in its final year, when I was in the fourth grade, the school had only two pupils—Howard Tate, an eighth grader, and me, a fourth grader. Howard's graduation left me the only youngster of school age in the camp. Mother fought like a tigress and almost overpowered board members of Olney School District No. 25 in her fight to get them to continue the school at least another year.

The board was on the verge of reversing its decision to close the school when one of them happened to mention the fact that what they were contemplating was in effect hiring a private tutor for me at a salary of one hundred dollars a month. Upon reappraisal none of the board was of the opinion that even by stretching the public school concept to the very extreme of its original intent should I be entitled to private tutoring.

"You big old dummy," Mother fumed at the hapless member who had voiced the private-tutor remark. The board, uneasy but firm, stuck to its guns. The year was 1922 and that was the fall Mother and I moved to Seaside so I could continue school.

In addition to being what Mother labeled "cowardly and stubborn," the board was pretty stuffy about spending taxpayers' money on interior appointments and frills. The Western Cooperage furnished the building, while the school district provided the basic essentials, which included a desk and a chair for the teacher, a dozen desks and seats of assorted sizes for pupils, a half-dozen wall maps, a blackboard but no chalk, and a stove.

Restrooms were two moss-covered outhouses half-hidden by underbrush and of a design and capacity proved and used by every family in camp. On rainy days to avoid a clothes-wetting trot to the outhouse we boys often just skipped around a corner to the lee side of the school. Mother found out about this handy but untidy practice and suggested that the other mothers order their sons to cease and desist.

Mrs. Johnson, in one of her jolly moods, told Mother her Fen and Jake didn't have to go to all that trouble. Mother wanted to know why. Mrs. Johnson said that already each had a length of "hangdown" long enough to reach from the school to the boys' outhouse. She slapped her thighs in uproarious laughter when Mother didn't seem to grasp her meaning.

"What's a hangdown?" Mother asked Dad that night at supper. A forkload of mashed potatoes dropped from his mouth and landed with a kerplunk on his plate. He sent me outside to the piped water supply to get a cold pitcher of water. When I returned Mother was the color of a boiled beet and Dad had tears in his eyes which I suspected were caused by laughing.

Restroom habits of the school's male population were among the district's minor problems. The rat and mouse population that congregated in the attic in winter was a far more serious threat to health than the few boys who now and then satisfied nature's call alongside the school building. The rats and mice didn't even bother to step outside the building. Sometimes droppings and liquids from the attic rodent population would dribble down into the classroom. And on hot days the odor that seeped down was nauseating. That was probably one of the reasons the teacher on warm days was always willing to let us study outside.

To expect us kids and the teacher to endure such degradation and filth was inhuman, Mother declared. It was worse than having to sit under an outhouse, Mrs. Johnson joined in. It would take more than a Pied Piper of Hamelin to rid the school attic of its mice and rats. In its time of need the camp turned to Fen Johnson. He was boosted up through the small attic entrance in the ceiling. A lighted kerosene lantern, a single barrel shotgun, and a box of shells followed. Fen's instructions were to fire away at glistening eyes or scurrying forms revealed by the light of the lantern.

Fen's first volley opened up an eight-inch hole in one end of the attic. Succeeding blasts sent several areas of the cedar-shaked roof rocketing skyward. By the time Fen ran out of shells there was enough daylight streaming into the attic from shotgun holes in the roof and gables to read a book by. Although the experiment didn't eliminate the rodent problem it did reduce it for a time and opened the way for new programs. One discovery was that with holes in the roof and the gables half-blown out there was free air circulation and no longer any unsavory odor.

Volunteer fathers patched the roof but instead of covering all the gable-end openings they screened a few so that air could continue to circulate through the attic. This removed the smell and also seemed to improve the heating ability of the big stove located near the center of the room.

As a final gesture to show man's superiority over rats and mice, lye water was sprinkled liberally throughout the attic. Next, the screened openings in the gables were temporarily sealed and several pans of liquid ammonia were set out. The school was closed for almost a week while the ammonia fumes did their work.

Dozens of the more stubborn rats and mice were overcome by the fumes and died patriotic deaths in defense of their homes. But hundreds fled the attic and sought new opportunities in rotted stumps, logs and brush in and beyond the schoolyard.

The camp dads then went to work sealing every visible crack and hole in the building with pieces of tin. "Them that is in will have to stay in and them that is out will have to stay out," was the way Daddy Hoyt explained the camp strategy.

With the rat problem not solved, but at least under control, another arose. A family of skunks set up housekeeping in one of the log skids under the school. Mother took the problem of the skunks before the school board. One of the members came out to the camp to have a look but after one deep breath he declared this was a matter that would have to be handled at the local level and definitely did not concern the school board. The only advice he had to offer, and it wasn't official, was that it might be wise for us kids to tiptoe in and out of school and not make any sudden loud noises which would frighten the skunks and cause them to really smell up the place.

The smell of skunk was so strong on several occasions that the teacher had to dismiss school. Dad was of the opinion that the mother skunk was probably in the family way and short tempered and nervous. He modified that opinion somewhat after he caught Fen and Jake pitching rocks under the schoolhouse. He ordered them both to crawl part way under the building. Fen could wheedle Mother, but in the words of

Fen, "Dad looked meaner than a wildcat with worms." Both boys crawled.

Later Mrs. Johnson came over to our house to have a say. One look at Dad and she suddenly had the urge to remain quiet. "Where's Fen and Jake?" Dad finally asked so she'd feel free to talk.

"They's bare-assed and settin' in the creek," she answered, eyes flashing and mouth tight-lipped.

"Seems a mite chilly for swimmin'," observed Dad dryly.

"They's not swimmin' and you damn well know it, Sam Churchill," she finally flared. "I've a good mind to send them over here and stink you out of *your* house," she added.

"If I ever hear of your boys throwing rocks at them skunks again it'll be you who'll go under the schoolhouse," Dad warned. Their eyes locked in double glares. Mrs. Johnson finally weakened and dropped her gaze. Some instinct for survival warned her what Mother and I already knew— Dad wasn't fooling.

Actually, Fen and Jake weren't too unhappy at first smelling like skunks for all of one school week. They idled away the isolation period hunting and fishing and smelling up the woods. The entire camp was off limits to them so they couldn't run errands. Before the week was up they got a real hankering to return to school. They'd sit moodily at the edge of the schoolhouse clearing watching us at recess and at noon hour playtimes.

With Fen and Jake no longer bothering them the skunk family became good neighbors. The teacher recruited them for a class in nature study. We'd gather grubs and worms for them and sneak raw eggs and milk from home. If there were ever any young ones we never saw them. But the two adults got so they'd come and go at will and at times would edge up cautiously and accept sweets held in our hands.

Between the classroom interruptions caused by the rats and mice and then by the skunks we weren't getting much school-work done.

"The only thing left is for a bear to wander into the classroom," the teacher with a resigned shrug said to Mother one day. The camp couldn't provide such an exceptional thrill but it did the next best thing—a bear cub in the schoolyard.

Mother again appeared before the school board. "We no longer have a school at the Western Cooperage camp," she complained, "we have a zoo."

Dad reprimanded Mother sternly for bothering the school board with such trifles.

"A live bear in the schoolyard is no trifle," she insisted.

Frankly, the little fellow didn't cause a ripple of excitement or concern with anyone except Mother. He apparently had somehow gotten separated from his mother. Attracted to the camp by the noise and cookhouse odors, he'd stumbled into the schoolhouse clearing by accident. At least that was how the men of the camp reconstructed the events leading up to his unscheduled visit.

I think it was Bert Hathaway, stepson of T. W. Robinson, the camp superintendent, who first noticed him. Next to Fen and Jake Johnson, Bert probably spent more time staring dreamily out the schoolhouse windows than anyone. Bert, incidentally, is now an oil distributor in Huntington Park, California. Bert hissed the word that there was a baby bear sniffing around the yard. The rest of us, including the teacher, scrambled for a peep spot at the two side windows. The bear heard the commotion. Bears have notoriously poor eyesight but a highly sensitive sense of smell. In an effort to pinpoint the source of scrambling feet, the little fellow reared up on his hind legs like a department store Teddy bear, suddenly curious and come to life.

Ignoring the protests of the teacher Bert and Fen and Jake sneaked out the back door that opened out to the woodshed where wood slabs for the school's heating stove were kept. Their plan was to circle the little fellow, confuse him, and capture him. They confused him but instead of cowering in fright he bolted for the school and skittered underneath between the log skids. Mr. and Mrs. Skunk resisted the intrusion. Within seconds the little bear came rolling and tumbling into view, pawing at his face and eyes and yowling and smelling like a barrelful of skunk concentrate.

Fen, Jake, and Bert lost all interest in capturing him. The rest of us came bounding out of the schoolroom as the skunk odor began taking over.

The last we saw of the little fellow he was on his feet and tearing headlong through the underbrush bawling to high heaven for his mother. I couldn't help but wonder if his mother would make him sit naked in Klaskanine Creek as Mrs. Johnson did with Fen and Jake when they came home after a much less serious encounter with these same two skunks.

School had to be recessed several more days while the classroom aired out.

"If I didn't know better I'd somehow suspect Fen and Jake Johnson of being at the bottom of all this," Mother said to Dad.

"And how do you know they ain't?" asked Dad.

If the poor old Western Cooperage school wasn't plagued by outside disturbances it would be hit by a siege of internal disorders. Winter snows were a continual problem. Wind-driven snow would seep in under the shake roof and pile in little drifts in the attic. Heat, boiling up from the panting stove, would melt the snow. The result was a continual dripping on pupils, books, desks, and papers until the attic snow melted away. These little disturbances on occasion forced a temporary recess of classes. Fen and Jake were responsible for some of these unscheduled holidays from school and it was rather clever the way they planned them.

Fen and Jake were the official fire tenders. They volunteered for the job, which was rather unusual considering their dislike for responsibility and work. I found out later they had a twofold purpose in volunteering. One was that the frequent trips to the woodshed for wood gave them a chance to spit. Throughout most of the school day both of them nursed a cud of tobacco.

Fen told me it was Jake who got the other idea, which was to keep the big oval-shaped stove piping hot when there was snow in the attic. On damp, rainy days when a chill from the ocean hung over the camp it was almost impossible to get Fen and Jake to keep a brisk fire in the stove except at moments when it was necessary to empty their mouths of tobacco juice.

But with a good snowfall and the likelihood that there was snow in the attic it was just as difficult to keep them in their seats. They would make a dozen trips a day to the woodshed, each time filling the stove to the brim with pitch knots and other heat-producing wood material that would turn the stove and its stovepipe to a cherry red in color.

In no time at all the schoolroom would become a bake oven. The teacher would order the door and windows opened and suggest to Fen and Jake that they close the stove draft and damper and use less wood. But by then it would be too late. The rising inferno of heat would have been at work melting snow in the attic. Pretty soon there would be the constant drip of water from above and the teacher, perplexed and agitated by this "Act of God" interruption, would announce school was dismissed for the rest of the day.

Mother never caught on to this little trick of Fen and Jake's. She thought they kept a roaring fire in the stove in hopes of burning the school down.

Unkept and crude as it was, the little Western Cooperage school provided us with sound basics in reading, writing, language, and arithmetic. There was also geography and spelling and those special categories of application and deportment that Mother watched with alertness.

Each teacher had her own favorites that she would add to the curriculum by writing them in ink in blank spaces on our report cards. Miss Della Brown, my first-grade teacher, added phonics and physiology to our first-grade studies. Marguerite Pinnell, who came the following year and had me in the second grade, added neatness. It was indicative because she ended up at the Hearst Ranch at San Simeon, California, and brought order and continuity to the late publisher's vast collection of art and artifacts. She is still there as of this writing. Another teacher, Violet Olson, is married and lives in Seattle, Washington. She is the daughter of the Olsons who ran the hotel at Olney.

My favorite, and the one whom I fell head over heels in love with, was Edith M. Hoskins, but by the time she arrived on the scene, school enrollment had dropped to two, Howard Tate and myself. It was a particularly good year for reasons other than Miss Hoskins. The school term was a bare eight months which meant I had an extra long summer vacation.

The camp fathers and school board may have been a little stuffy about such things as spending time or money to nail up loose boards, replace broken windowpanes, or repair the porch and steps of the school building. But when it came to selecting a teacher they were as thorough as a judge at the Miss America pageant. Mother tried to direct their eyes and decisions toward some of the older, more mature women with a few years of classroom teaching to their credit. But the board would have none of that.

"A woman don't have to look like a hemlock tree to have brains," one of the board members told her. The board's selection was not always unanimous but it always leaned toward the Miss Oregon figures and Hey Daddy faces. This was at a time when high school graduates with a teacher's certificate could teach in country schools.

"If you men get them any younger they won't be as old as some of the boys in the school," Mother warned. Mother wasn't too far from zeroing in on the truth. Some of the older boys in school were almost the size of men. Discipline was as delicate as the hairspring in a watch.

Fen and Jake Johnson had the bad habit of wandering off

at recess and maybe not showing up again for a day or two. Bert Hathaway liked a leisurely noon hour. On the dot of eleven each day he'd get up from his seat, excuse himself, and go home to lunch.

Mother spent half her days scouting the creek banks and fishing holes looking for Fen and Jake or trying to talk Bert into going home at twelve o'clock for lunch the same as we little kids.

"You're setting a very bad example," Mother would point out.

"But I get hungry early," Bert would answer.

The problem solved itself eventually when the three of them finally graduated.

## Chapter 10

## FUN ON THE RUN

Big Ben was boss at the Western Cooperage camp. Big Ben was the favorite brand of alarm clock. One of Dad's nightly rituals before retiring was winding Big Ben, making certain the alarm was set for 4:30 A.M., and pulling out the pin at the rear of the clock so that the alarm would go off at the appointed hour.

At the first crash of the alarm next morning Dad's feet would thump against the thin throw rug that covered the cold wood floor on his side of the bed. Lighting the kerosene lamp that sat on the dresser in the lean-to bedroom, he would come into the main house, where I slept, and head for the kitchen stove at one end of the room. There were no wasted moments at 4:30 o'clock of a winter morning with a foot of snow outside and ice in the teakettle inside.

Pounding his bare feet against the icy-cold wall-to-wall linoleum to keep the circulation going, he'd next douse a liberal amount of kerosene on the shavings and kindling that had been placed in the stove firebox the night before. A touch of flame from a husky-stemmed, strike-it-anywhere match and the old stove would come to life.

While the stove was doing its best to drive the early morning chill from the room Dad would be ducking out of his nightshirt and into the long wool underwear which loggers wore winter and summer. In quick succession he next donned heavy wool socks, shirt, and work overalls held in place by sturdy, broad-banded suspenders. On rainy days the woods garb was usually tin pants (a heavy, stiff material sometimes treated with paraffin or some other waxy material that made the pants stiffer than ever, but more water resistant) and a jacket-like coat of the same material.

Except for the cooks, who were usually up by 3 A.M. lighting the big wood-burning ranges and getting breakfast started for the fifty or so bachelor loggers living in bunkhouses, Dad was the first man in camp to roll out of bed. On Sundays, an accepted day of rest for loggers in camps from Maine to Northern California, Dad would lie in bed and toss and sigh until 5 A.M.

Once he was up and dressed and had the fire going it was pretty difficult for anyone else to sleep or oversleep because Dad would clump around like a flat-footed elephant and usually start to sing. It wasn't singing such as Enrico Caruso might have indulged in. I've since suspected that Dad had a bit of Elvis Presley or England's Beatles in him. He snorted his words a bit like Elvis, but the over-all noise level was louder than the best efforts of the Beatles.

I also suspect that his morning musical clamor was a subtle reminder for Mother to get up and prepare breakfast. If that was the purpose, it worked. Each morning as Mother would stumble from the bedroom addition in nightgown and robe, blinking like an owl in the lamplight, Dad always greeted her with a cheery, "Well now, are you awake?"

"No, I'm not," Mother would sometimes announce, "but it's impossible to sleep."

The smell of fried pork, eggs, oven toast, hotcakes, or hot cereal usually was more than I could ignore so I'd get up and we'd all have breakfast together. Breakfast finished, Dad would put on his heavy calk-soled shoes, give Mother and me a peck of a kiss on the cheek and head up the railroad track toward the machine shop where the crew train that hauled the men out to the logging area sat ready and waiting with steam up and headlight cutting a yellow shaft through the darkness.

As soon as the locomotive got under way with its string

of logging cars and men, Mother and I would make a dash for our respective beds.

At the tag end of the day the pattern would be reversed. It would be Mother and I who wanted to sit up and talk and were wide awake. Sometimes by eight o'clock and never later than nine, Dad would bank the wood fire in the heating stove so it would last at least part of the night, make a nest of kindling and shavings in the cookstove, pick up the lamp, and shoo us off to bed.

Nine o'clock was the magic hour in the Western Cooperage camp. By that time most every man, woman, and child was in bed. The only sounds would be the night chatter of Klaskanine Creek, the gossip of a few frogs, the sigh of the wind around the eaves of the house, and possibly the questioning "Whoooo?" of a night prowling owl.

The next morning Big Bens in a dozen homes would rout heads of families from the warm coziness of their beds and the camp would be alive and vibrant for another fourteen to sixteen hours.

We weren't devoid of social activities and entertainment. Dad and Mother might take me along and visit the Mel Tates across the track. Mr. Tate had run locomotives for a number of big logging outfits in Washington and Oregon and he was good company. On these visits he'd usually go into a back room and return with a bottle of elderberry wine. At other times two or three families might get together and play cards, or if they were at our house, play the Victor talking machine and sing.

Now and then on special occasions there would be programs by the pupils at the schoolhouse, or more elaborate ones, such as the Christmas pageant directed by Mother, in the cookhouse dining room. But no matter what the activity it usually ended fairly early so that the work-weary logger husbands could be home and in bed by 9 P.M.

Summer was more relaxed and people were more eager to do things. One of the big events at this time of the year were the Saturday night dances in the attic of the Olsons' warehouse at Olney. Dad didn't know how to dance but Uncle Marsh was a hell raiser on a dance floor. Dad and Mother and Uncle Marsh and Aunt Blanche would sometimes attend the warehouse dances.

They usually lasted all night. We kids would be bedded down in blankets at one end of the big hall-like attic. Habit was strong with Dad and dance or no dance he usually would settle down on a bench and drop off into a sound sleep, sitting up, by ten o'clock; or as Uncle Marsh used to say, "Before there'd even been one fight."

Following the dance everyone would hurry over to the Olney hotel for one of Mrs. Olson's hearty breakfasts. After that there was usually a baseball game between a team of Western Cooperage loggers and one from Olney. Five-Fingered Frenchy, the brakeman, organized the Western Cooperage team. Both sides had some pretty sharp ball players, including Frenchy whose missing fingers didn't seem to interfere one bit with his fielding, throwing, or batting.

Mike O'Farrell was pitcher for the Olney team. They were an elite bunch with suits and everything and had whipped a professional team from Astoria several times.

After the all-night dance it sometimes took a little while for several of the team members to sober up enough to be in playing condition, but once the game got under way it kept going the rest of the day.

The most difficult spot to fill was that of umpire. It took a special brand of courage to tell a fellow like Uncle Marsh that after three perfectly pitched balls over the plate he was out and it was time for a new batter. I remember one time when it took three men to hold Uncle Marsh and keep him from ending the game ahead of time by disposing of the umpire. They finally got him quieted down by telling him that hitting the umpire would be a cowardly act because he had only one eye.

"Then tell the sonofabitch to open his good eye and quit

using his bad eye," Uncle Marsh roared. Aunt Blanche had a little talk with Uncle Marsh on the way home that night, and that ended his baseball career.

Following a Saturday night dance and Sunday baseball game at Olney, Monday was usually a poor work day in the woods and things sometimes didn't get back to normal until about Wednesday.

Logging was a hurry-up business and the exuberance and excitement generated by the throbbing machines, whining cables, and bounding logs carried over into off-work pleasures and activities.

That's why the Olney dances and baseball games were such fun. They usually spawned a half-dozen or dozen fights. The average dance couldn't generate enough action to sustain the average logger for very long. His spirits would start to drag and he would be impelled to stir up a little action on his own. The handiest materials were his imagination and his own two fists.

A couple of Western Cooperage loggers were having a go-around one Sunday afternoon down at the crossing. A dozen or so spectators, including myself and two or three other kids, were standing around watching. Mother strolled down to see what was going on. Finding that it was a fight, and that I was watching, and worst of all, enjoying it, she became incensed. Pushing through the circle of idlers watching the two fighters, she wanted to know, "Why are you two fighting?"

The two men stared in bewilderment at Mother, then shifted their gazes to each other. One finally blurted out: "My God, Mrs. Churchill, do we have to have a reason?"

The incident reveals much about the character, spirit, and philosophy of the average logger of that period. He was a gifted, personable, reckless individual whose life force was action. Pour him a drink and he would gulp it down. Give him two courses of action and he'd make an immediate choice. His choice might not be the better of the two but it was quick and it was final.

Some of this restless energy and exuberance that gripped our fathers rubbed off on us. It was well that it did for ours was an uncluttered childhood in which play and fun were activities of one's own choosing. There was no make-believe world of movies, radio, or television to entertain us. In the whole of the Western Cooperage camp there wasn't a single football or basketball and our only association with baseball was the games we saw now and then at Olney.

There were no retail stores to wander through; no heated swimming pools, boys' clubs, or social centers. And there were no neglected children or broken homes. By present standards we were underprivileged. But there were no paid social workers to tell us and our parents that we were, so we lived each day to the fullest—loved, happy, carefree, and unenvious.

The joys and fulfillments of logging-camp living weren't always apparent to outsiders. One of Mother's sisters, visiting us from the East, was appalled at the isolation and lack of services and of such minimum conveniences as a bath tub or, in fact, any indoor plumbing.

"Samuel is being reared in a vacuum," she said disgustedly one night after heating water in the copper washboiler on top of the stove for a bath in a galvanized washtub.

"With God so close you can feel His presence, and with the abundance and beauty of nature on every hand, how can you possibly believe that?" Mother challenged.

I don't know how the discussion ended because I was ordered into the built-on bedroom with Dad while Aunt Sue undressed and bathed. I could hear mother giggling as she watched Aunt Sue trying to squeeze all of herself into the limited space of the circular washtub. I knew without looking she wasn't having much success. Only little fellows of my age and size could get all the way in. Adults had to half squat, or sit with their feet in the tub and their behinds on the rim. From the hurried splashings and groans of discomfort I suspected Aunt Sue had finally decided to sit on the rim.

She remained with us for almost a month and by the time she returned to her husband and family in Boston she was willing to concede to Mother that the Western Cooperage community had its good points. She supervised installation of a big rope swing on the brow of a slope overlooking the camp. The swing support was a length of sapling held in place by heavy limbs of two adjoining trees. That was almost fifty years ago and the swing and its supporting crossbeam, and even the camp, are long gone. But the two trees are still there.

Aunt Sue was sharp-tongued and brusque and older than Mother. After she and the camp residents sort of got to know each other they liked each other. The swing idea made her a favorite with us kids. We all did our best to please her and let her know, without actually saying so, that she had been accepted as one of us. But she sometimes taxed our patience and understanding.

There was the time she gave Jake Johnson a sound whipping. That alone was enough to endear her to the camp forever, even though she later had to apologize to Jake and the Johnsons because it was all a mistake.

On the day of the whipping I was up in the top of a forty-foot-tall sapling and Jake was on the ground with an ax chopping it down. It was an old Western Cooperage sport and the worst that could happen would be a few broken bones. The idea was for the party in the tree to ride it to the ground when it fell. You maneuvered yourself so that you were on the topside of the trunk when it hit, and not on the underside between the trunk and the ground. The limbs cushioned the landing jar.

Aunt Sue didn't understand all these safety precautions and she most assuredly didn't know Jake and I were just having some routine fun. When she saw Jake chopping down the tree I was in, she let out a holler that must have reached the logging area beyond Camp 2. From my perch in the top of the tree I could see her storming through the underbrush toward us.

"Aunt Sue's coming to watch," I yelled down at Jake. He began chopping faster so as to send me whooshing toward the ground about the time Aunt Sue would arrive. Then it would be my turn to chop and let him ride a tree to the ground.

I was as astonished as Jake when Aunt Sue grabbed him by the scruff of his neck and began flailing his legs and backside with a length of broken limb she had picked up on the way. Jake made a leap for the tree I was in but Aunt Sue went to work on his unprotected rear with such vigor that he gave up and dropped back to the ground.

About this time there was a loud snapping of wood at the base of the tree where Jake had been chopping. There was a dizzy, exhilarating feeling as the top swayed and began tipping, lazily, toward the ground. "Watch out below," I shouted. Aunt Sue looked up and with a horrified "Merciful God in heaven," crumpled into a dead faint. By the time the tree landed and I had followed the trunk back to the stump and Jake and Aunt Sue, she had recovered. She looked a little glassy-eyed and her breathing came in sighs and gasps but she was sitting up and staring at Jake and me with a look of wonder.

There was mutual interest. It was the first time either Jake or I had seen anyone faint. "Is it like dying?" Jake wanted to know. Aunt Sue said she wasn't certain and for Jake to take his ax, go home and chop wood, and stop asking silly questions. We told her that wouldn't be fair because it was Jake's turn to ride a tree and my turn to chop. She said she just didn't feel like any more chopping at the moment and maybe we could play some other game. Jake suggested maybe we could have a foot race across the county road bridge that crossed Klaskanine Creek by his house.

Aunt Sue said that sounded much more reasonable and she would go along and be judge. I thought she was going to faint again when she found we did our racing not on the roadway of the bridge but on the two by six planks that ran along the top of the bridge railing. She leaned over the railing and looked down the twenty feet or so to the boulder-strewn creek bed. She said she had a better idea, and to follow her. She took us up to the camp commissary and bought us each a Centennial chocolate with white cream filling. Centennial chocolates came in a little brown box and were the most luxurious candy in the whole world. They cost a nickel and I think it was the first Centennial Jake had ever eaten.

"Your aunt scares easy," he commented while savoring the creamy goodness of this unexpected candy delight, "but she's nice."

Mother and Dad knew about the tree riding and other games and activities of camp youngsters, but they hadn't known about the bridge racing until Aunt Sue told them. I was sternly forbidden ever to run, or even walk, the bridge railings again.

"I s'pose she told them about the trestle too," lamented Jake. She hadn't, but I had a feeling she would have had she known about it. The trestle was a towering structure that at one time had carried a railroad spur line ninety feet above the floor of a canyon. The ties and rails had been taken up a year or so previous, leaving only the log stringers to provide a narrow footpath high over the canyon. It was used by Western Cooperage youngsters to see if a boy was ready to graduate to the worldly cares and responsibilities of manhood. The test was simple enough. A candidate, anxious to prove he was now a man, had only to run full tilt along the log path. A slip or misstep meant a ninety-foot fall and probable instant death in the tangle of logs, stumps, rocks and underbrush below. For safety in running the old bridge, shoes and socks were removed to reduce the risk of slipping on the barkless, weather-glazed surface of the old logs.

The manhood test was a closely guarded secret. There was mutual agreement among us young folks that parents and other adults in the camp might be upset if they knew of it and the part the abandoned railroad trestle had in it.

Phil Peets almost gave the secret away. He stumbled and fell during his first test. Luckily it was right at the start so he only fell ten or fifteen feet and collected a few minor bruises and scratches. His mother was mildly curious but not overly so. Cuts, bruises, and scratches were normal reminders of a happy, industrious, and eventful day.

Phil was getting a reputation for being a little unsteady on his feet. A few weeks prior to his trestle mishap he tumbled from the railing of the county road bridge. He was in bed a couple of days with a lump the size of a doorknob on his forehead.

"It's a miracle he wasn't killed," said Mother, shaking a finger at me across the supper table as though I'd maybe tripped him. She and Dad then warned me never to play on or around high trestles. Especially abandoned ones, said Dad, because they were often rotted and near collapse. And at best they offered skimpy, insecure footing.

I said I wouldn't think of playing on scary old trestles.

"Is that a promise?" asked Mother.

I suddenly felt very guilty and anxious to talk about something besides trestles. "I promise," I said. That ended the subject because at our house a promise was a promise. It was the same as telling God face to face that you would or would not do something.

I was thankful that Jake had already introduced me to the Manhood Trestle and that I had raced across it and passed the manhood test. Passing the manhood test was of major importance to success, acceptance, and peace of mind in the Western Cooperage camp.

## Chapter 11

## STEAMBOAT ON THE COLUMBIA

Two or three times a year Mother would pack a bag and off we'd go to Portland for two or three days for what she termed "Shopping, a change of scenery, and manners."

Upon our return to camp from such a trip I was the center of attraction for several days, recounting the sights and sounds of a city where one downtown building had more people working in it than lived and worked in the whole Western Cooperage camp.

Portland in those days was a bewildering metropolis of some one hundred thousand persons and to me it seemed that all one hundred thousand were often on the streets all at the same time.

There were buildings as tall as two fir trees, one on top of the other. And it was noisier than a half-dozen Humboldt yarders all going at once.

It was almost unbelievable the conveniences that city folks took for granted. Push a button and on went the electric lights. The outhouse was inside and taking a bath was so easy that Mother and I would sometimes take as many as two a day on our visits.

There were reminders on every hand that Portland was an offspring of the big timber country. Smoke boiled skyward night and day from a dozen mills clustered along water sites in and approaching the city. The steady stream of river boats leaving and arriving were well laden with men and supplies going to and from the hundreds of logging camps whose lifelines reached to ports of call along the Washington

and Oregon shores of the Columbia River. Teams of grunting tugboats hustled rafts of logs upstream from the Columbia to the Willamette and through the heart of the city to
waiting mills on the outskirts.

On these visits to Portland there was usually a sentimental
trip to the Union Station where Dad and Mother stepped
from the train in 1911 and where Dad arrived alone in 1902.
We'd stand on the Broadway Bridge approach and look down
on the busy hordes of switch engines puffing on various
errands about the railroad yards.

"The steel sinews that bind a nation," is how Mother described railroads. "Those rails can take you from here to
anywhere in the United States," Mother used to remind me,
"even to Boston." Sometimes as we watched and talked about
the railroad there would be a touch of longing in her voice
at the mention of Boston or other far East points, but she
would quickly repulse any attack of homesickness with a
brusque "You've seen your trains, now let's go shopping."

Shopping with Mother was an ordeal of blistered feet and
endless waiting. For every item purchased she would spend
what seemed hours just looking, fingering, musing, and ex-
claiming.

"I've got to store up enough looking in three days to last
six months," she used to explain cheerfully.

The real excitement of a visit to Portland, for me at least,
was getting there. These days, by surfaced highway and auto-
mobile, it's an easy three-hour drive from the old camp site
to downtown Portland. During my boyhood, by rutted dirt
and rock road and jolting, straining Buick or Studebaker, it
took that long to drive from camp to Astoria. There were no
Greyhound-type bus schedules. Whenever there were
enough camp residents to make a carload for the trip a for-
hire car would be sent out the twenty miles from Astoria.
The cars were usually equipped with jump seats in the leg
space normally reserved for back seat passengers. Addition
of the jump seats, an uncomfortable folding-type, would

boost passenger capacity from a crowded seven to a sardine-fit of ten. Luggage and loggers' packs and calked boots were lashed on the outside to fenders, hood, and the spare tire rack at the rear.

I was nine years old before I knew the Western Cooperage–Astoria jitney had cushions. Every trip I bounced along on somebody's lap.

Two flat tires were average for the twenty-mile trip. No flat tires was almost unheard of. Three were not unusual and I have seen the time when an overloaded bus would have a full round of flats including the spare. Each flat necessitated everyone untangling arms and legs and getting out of the car while it was jacked up for repairs. The bus operators often carried two spares. This saved time and tempers in case of flats but after two flats, which would place both spares in service, tubes had to be patched on the road and the tire reinflated with a hand pump.

Many loggers preferred hitching a ride on the logging train from camp to Olney and hiking the ten miles from Olney to Astoria. It was cheaper, less bother, "and a damnsight faster" most of the time, Uncle Marshall claimed. The faithful little *Teddy Roosevelt*, the one-cylindered gasoline launch that had carried Dad and Mother from Astoria to Olney on their honeymoon trip in 1911 was still operating but much too leisurely for most of the eager, town-hungry loggers.

Once you got to Astoria there were two commercial means of getting on to Portland—by river steamer or by railroad train. Sometimes we took the train to please me. More often we went by riverboat to please Mother. She was a bit of a favorite with many of the river crews since many of them had heard the story of how she took over the wheel of the *Teddy Roosevelt* and showed the pilot how to steer a smoother course through choppy water.

The boat trip took about seven hours from Astoria with the route up the Columbia River ninety miles or so to the confluence of the Willamette and up the Willamette a dozen miles or more to the downtown terminal dock in Portland.

"And how's the Western Cooperage's favorite lady pilot?" Captain L. O. Hosford of the *Georgiana* would call out if he happened to see us coming aboard.

"Ready to take over the minute some of these landlubber captains retire," Mother would shout back amid chuckles and hand waves from crew members.

"That'll be the day when even the salmon will clear out of the river," Captain Hosford would roar back in mock disgust that usually ended in a roll of belly laughter. Sometimes, if he had a spare moment, Captain Hosford would personally escort Mother and me to a seat beside one of the big view windows in the enclosed lounge.

"Ma'm," he'd say with feigned gruffness, pointing to the five or six miles of open water between us and the Washington shore, "there's enough water out there to float the whole city of Boston."

"And the only ones who know how to steer a proper course on it are Indians and fish," Mother would snap, trying hard to hold back the grin that always tugged at the corners of her mouth when she was having a go-around with Captain Hosford.

Captain Hosford and the *Georgiana* were Mother's special favorites on the Columbia River. Sometimes, though, we'd take the night boat, the *Lurline*. It was a freighter with cabin facilities for overnight passengers. It left Astoria about 7 P.M. and arrived in Portland early the following morning. I liked sleeping in a bunk and dreamily listening to the throb of the engines and the slap of river swells against the wooden hull, but the disappointing thing about night travel on the river was that you couldn't see anything.

The *Georgiana*, on the other hand, was sort of a Churchill family pet. It was big enough so that Dad could ride it to Portland without getting seasick. And it was just about my age. A handsome craft painted a spotless white from the water line up, it was powered by a propeller instead of the

16. A high-climber, with his saw dangling from his belt, has just finished topping a giant Douglas fir which will be rigged as a spar tree. He made ten dollars a day for such work.

17. The high-lead block above this climber weighed almost a ton.

18. Logs being brought in on a skyline used to bridge canyons or move timber down steep slopes. *(Photograph courtesy of the Mallory Logging Equipment Company, Portland, Oregon)*

19. Big timber required heavy equipment, as illustrated by the size of these high-lead blocks. Some weighed well *over* a ton.

20. A typical logging scene in the early days. The donkey engine at the left, called a swing donkey, dragged logs to the railroad where they were loaded onto cars by the loading donkey at the right. *(Photo courtesy of Ball Studio, Astoria, Oregon)*

22. A logging locomotive high in the wooded ridges of Oregon.

21. Steel spar skidders were introduced about 1915 and did away with the use of trees as spars. *(Photograph courtesy of the Mallory Logging Equipment Company, Portland, Oregon)*

. Building a logging railroad tres-
the hard way with a steam pile
iver. *(Kenneth Long Photo)*

24. An example of logger engineering—
part of a ninety-foot-high trestle.

25. A typical scene at a logging camp log dump where railroad cars unloaded into water so that the logs could be assembled in rafts and towed to the mill. (*Photograph courtesy of the Mallory Logging Equipment Company, Portland, Oregon*)

cumbersome stern paddle wheel used by most of the other boats on the Lower Columbia run. She tipped the scales at 261 tons and under the stern eyes of Captain Hosford was kept as spic and span as a private yacht.

On the upriver trip to Portland the *Georgiana* left Astoria shortly after noon and would be in Portland early that same evening. One-way fare was one dollar.

The daylight trip up the Columbia to the Willamette and on to Portland usually turned out to be a history lesson for me with Mother the teacher. There was Grays Bay, upriver a few miles from Astoria and on the Washington State side, where Captain Robert Gray of the ship *Columbia* dropped anchor on a May day in 1792.

I was always reminded, too, that the exploration party headed by Meriwether Lewis and William Clark paddled down these same waters in 1805 and holed up for the winter in a log fort with stockade that they named Fort Clatsop. The site of the old fort was across Youngs Bay from Astoria on the banks of Lewis and Clark River.

Whenever we were in Astoria I was reminded constantly that even the restrooms in the Beehive department store were on hallowed ground. It was very likely, said Mother, that almost any place you walked, sat, or spit on in Astoria had been walked, sat, and spit on more than one hundred years earlier by men of John Jacob Astor's Pacific Fur Company. Building of old Fort Astoria had started in June of 1811 and there was a lot of Boston muscle behind the broadaxes that felled the trees and notched the logs for the stockade and living and storage quarters, Mother declared.

I don't know whether history has recorded any of that early Fort Astoria crew from Boston but no matter. Mother had a knack of putting a Bostonian in charge of every key achievement of United States history from Bunker Hill to the atomic bomb in World War II.

With Mother as guide I spent many an hour walking over rock and rubble between Fourteenth and Fifteenth streets on

Exchange Street a block from St. Mary's Hospital where I was born. Mother would pose like a Viking in the middle of the empty lot. "Remember this always, Samuel," she'd command. "On this very spot one hundred and five years ago the most western outpost of the United States of America was hewn from raw forest and a new world power was born."

At five years of age I had difficulty understanding why anyone would want to live in a log fort when he could go to the Weinhard Hotel a few blocks away and get a warm, comfortable room the same as Mother and I did for a reasonable price. It seemed to me the Weinhard Hotel must have been in Astoria forever, but Mother said not. She said until John Jacob Astor's Astorians came and built the fort there was nothing.

I double-checked this bit of information with Jake and Fen Johnson once and both of them rather agreed with me. Jake said Astoria had been there for as long as he could remember and Fen said the same thing. I asked if either of them had ever seen a fort near St. Mary's Hospital and both of them said no. It was hard for me to believe that maybe Mother was wrong about this fort business but it hardly seemed worth arguing about. The site is now properly marked so Mother must have been right.

Although I might not have exhibited much enthusiasm for events of the past, the boat trip up the Columbia was a front row seat of the wonders of the present. From the broad lap of the river one could sweep the crest of the Coast Range on both the Oregon and Washington shores. It seemed there was hardly a spot not marked by white puffs of steam and smoke from dozens and dozens of steam donkey engines tearing at the breathtaking expanse of virgin forest that rolled in endless dips and rumples from the shores of the river to far outdistance the eye.

It was a period of teeming activity on the Columbia. Steamboats, tugs, barges and other craft hurried on freight and passenger errands from Astoria east and north almost to the Canadian border.

Log rafts by the dozens, guided by sturdy little tugs, nosed from secluded sloughs and other convenient logging railroad unloading sites and headed for the never silent mills that stood almost within sight of each other along both the Oregon and Washington shores.

Smoke from the stacks of these same mills sometimes clung to the shoreline for a hundred miles. On night trips up the river the glow of their waste burners and dock lights outshone the feeble efforts of the towns of which the mills were supposedly only a part.

From the deck of the *Georgiana* this bewitching world of timber, smoke, and sawdust waste glided by as though on a hurried errand of its own. You get a truer picture of a land and its peoples observing them at a distance, Mother used to say. The deck of a boat in the middle of a river is an ideal vantage point from which to watch, analyze, and accurately appraise the world around you, Mother maintained.

The Columbia was awesomely magnificent as a study object itself. Originating twenty-six hundred feet above sea level in a wilderness spot walled by the western slope of the Canadian Rockies on one side and the scowling brow of the Selkirks on the other, it powered its way twelve hundred and ten uninterrupted miles from the Province of British Columbia to the Pacific Ocean. En route it flipped on its side and shot through a narrow, three-hundred-and-fifty-foot-deep trench a few miles below the ancient and historic Indian fishing falls of Celilo. Finding the Cascade Range directly in its path, it had torn a mammoth fifty-mile-long gorge through the backbone of this range and flowed on to the Pacific.

"It reminds me of your father," Mother used to say of the Columbia, "stubborn, reliable, and strong."

Dad never felt the kinship for the Columbia that Mother and I did. It was a distrust and lukewarmness probably born of his younger days on the log-filled waters of the Penobscot,

Saint Croix, and other Maine and Canadian streams during the turbulent log drives. But there was a measure of admiration and respect in his attitude toward the river. "I'm of no mind to like any river but if I was to it would be the Columbia," he once remarked while riding the *Georgiana* with us and staring at one of Simon Benson's log rafts.

One of Mr. Benson's ocean-going log rafts was a startling monster to happen across even in broad daylight. They were like nothing God nor man had ever before, or since, turned loose on the Columbia River. Almost ten times the size of an ordinary log raft, they dwarfed the 261 tons and 135-foot length of the sturdy little *Georgiana*.

"Benson's a fool," was the first reaction of almost every Columbia River logger, including Dad and Uncle Marsh, on meeting up with a Benson leviathan. Each raft is best described as a cigar-shaped bundle of logs eight hundred feet or more in length and bound together with one hundred and fifteen tons of chain and tons more of assorted cables.

The deck or top layer of logs humped thirteen feet above the surface of the water, almost eye level with passengers peering out lounge deck windows of the *Georgiana*. Bottom logs of the raft were twenty-six feet below the surface of the river.

A miniature island of logs, one of Mr. Benson's rafts, fifty-six feet in width amidships, had sufficient surface on which to anchor the Western Cooperage machine shop, cookhouse, office, and all the outhouses in camp.

Each raft contained from three and a half million to five million board feet, or in terms of live timber, logs, piling, spars, and other raw forest products from one hundred acres of timberland. A total of one hundred and twenty such rafts were built in Wallace Slough, near Clatskanie on the Lower Columbia, and towed by tug across the bar and south via the Pacific Ocean to San Diego, California. From the first such trip in 1906 to the last in 1941 only four of the great log giants were lost at sea. In late years some of the rafts were a thousand feet in length, held together by two hundred and seventy tons of chains, more than the total weight of the *Georgiana*. They were of such size they easily carried extra cargoes of poles, shingles, lath, and sawed lumber on each trip. It took some forty-two working days to build such a raft and fifteen to twenty days to tow it to San Diego.

A native of Norway who started logging with bull teams on the Lower Columbia as early as 1891, Simon Benson built his mill in San Diego on the hunch that the area would one day be a wide open market. He couldn't have been more right. Simon Benson is the only lumberman I know of with the temerity to build a mill eleven hundred miles from the land upon which his timber grew and was harvested. He did, and he made it pay, handsomely.

There was a lesson to be learned from the courage and success of Simon Benson, and Mother was persistent in pounding it home, especially to me.

"Anything a Simon Benson can do, you can do," she declared time and again whenever she imagined Dad and I needed some pushing. Whenever Mother would launch into one of her "Go get 'em" lectures as Uncle Marsh termed them, Dad would light the kerosene lantern and go outside for a walk. Or if it were daylight he'd go out to the woodshed and chop wood. So it was I who usually had to sit through Mother's pep talks. I sometimes wished we'd never seen one of Mr. Benson's seagoing rafts on the river. I think Big Sam sometimes secretly wished the same thing, although he never hinted as much.

The only time I felt any real interest or gratitude toward Mr. Benson was when Mother and I would be in downtown Portland and I'd suddenly get terribly thirsty. Mr. Benson had provided Portland with a number of four-armed, bronze drinking fountains located on various downtown street corners.

Mother was careful to point out that I was drinking from one of Mr. Benson's fountains. Some of the original fountains are still serving downtown shoppers in Portland. Whenever I bend over to drink from one I can almost hear Mother's voice reminding me as it did some forty-five years ago: "If Mr. Benson had been content to remain a common ordinary logger you'd still be thirsty."

The land, the river, and the people are no longer the same. The old night freighter *Lurline* left the river in 1935 and the *Georgiana* in 1939 was renamed the *Lake Bonneville* and shifted to an upriver tourist run from Portland to the smooth water reservoir behind Bonneville Dam where the Columbia used to roar and churn its way through its fifty-mile gorge.

The waters of Wallace Slough where Simon Benson used to build his giant rafts are quiet and unruffled except by tides and winds and stealthy river currents. The river no longer flips on its side and goes racing through its three-hundred-and-fifty-foot-deep trench. It and Celilo Falls, the ancient Indian fishing spot, are both buried under the backwaters of The Dalles Dam.

At Astoria between the Oregon and Washington shores they are building a bridge so that U. S. Highway 101 traffic will roll at sixty miles an hour across the five-mile width of water instead of moving leisurely by ferry.

The old stern wheelers and the *Georgiana*, that I rode as a boy, long ago passed on. The decks I walked are awash somewhere in the depths of time. Tankers, freighters, lumber ships, and other cargo carriers come coasting in over the bar from the Pacific and feel their way upstream toward sawmill docks, Portland, Vancouver, and other ports of call.

Diesel tugs push steel and wooden barges. There are log rafts but not in the numbers they used to be. The view from the river has changed. The great stands of virgin forest that swept from lowland to ridge in tides of green are no longer to be seen. A few remain but for the most part the hills are cropped and ugly, although on tens of thousands of acres each year new forest is being seeded and planted.

A few pilings, pushing out of the water at odd angles and

with willow and grass rooted and flourishing in the rotted
fibers of their once iron-hard sinews of wood, are solemn
reminders of a day in the past when dozens of logging railroads walked on trestles to log dumping sites along the river.
Trucks now do the hauling that the railroads and the *Lurlines*
and *Georgianas* used to do.

The river itself still pours one hundred and sixty million
acre-feet of water a year, drawn from two hundred and
fifty-nine thousand square miles of mountains and valleys in
the Pacific Northwest and Canada, into the Pacific Ocean.
That flood of free energy has since been harnessed by dams
to provide millions of kilowatts of electrical power for farms,
homes, and industry. It cools the forces of the sun held in
leash by giant reactors at the Hanford Atomic Works in
Washington State. Its cool, moist touch has transformed millions of acres of desert waste into lush, productive farms by
means of irrigation.

Although the great Columbia of today may seem quieter
and more relaxed than as I remember it as a boy, it isn't.
Some two thousand commercial fishing boats call it home,
these days. More than two hundred and fifty tugs and tow-
boats scurry about its broad, meandering surface on errands
of importance. At least two hundred deep-sea charter and
private craft churn through its waters. And moving sedately
among these skittering craft are hundreds of mysterious,
knowledgeable ocean craft ending or beginning trips that
may take products of Oregon's forests, farms, and industry
to waiting customers in ports of the world.

On the surface she is as big, as robust and as energetic as
ever. But under the surface, where the waters are quieter,
where rivers store their memories and recall the past and
maybe think about the future, I think you'll find sadness. I
think the Columbia at heart will always be a loggers' river.
She'll water desert farms, fill transmission lines with electrical
energy, cool the mighty reactors at Hanford, and let river
craft and ocean freighters inch at will along her lap. But I

think she longs for the days when Simon Benson's rafts used to nose out of Wallace Slough and head downstream toward the open sea. I think she misses the slap and splash of millions of board feet of logs tumbling into her arms each day from a half hundred logging railroads that reached inland as far as fifty or more miles to transport logs from cutting areas to tidewater dumping sites from which they could be floated to mills.

Gone is the pleasant, crunchy sound of calk shoes biting into wood; the hoots and hollers of that earlier logger breed exemplified by Big Sam and Uncle Marsh. There are no more friendly little wooden-hulled steamers with warning notices posted in their lounge and passenger sections: "No calk shoes allowed."

I think the river misses the men of fifty years ago who accepted her as she was, who didn't dam, harness, pollute, regulate, and restrict—men who cursed her rebellious moods when she'd send down floods of water and float away dockside stores of lumber and other cargo and do horrendous damage, but who loved her and were grateful for her long periods of gentleness and helpful moods.

I think the Columbia River misses all of these things of the past.

Or maybe it isn't the river at all.

Maybe it's just me.

## Chapter 12

# FIRE IN THE SKY

The morning of September 26, 1918, broke out of the east hot as a bake oven. The air was heavy and thick and dry as dust. A thin haze of smoke turned the white glare of the sun to a dull, coppery hue that gave the Western Cooperage camp an eerie, unnatural, and somber look.

It was to be a day of uneasiness, and a night of terror. I remember Mother remarking to Dad at breakfast about the unusual quiet. "Where are the birds?" she asked. It was as though God and Nature had suddenly walked off and left us.

I walked with Dad to the crew train that hauled the men to the logging area. On the way Jim Irving, Western Cooperage woods' boss, fell in step with us. A fleck of wood ash drifted down from the smoke haze above. Mr. Irving reached out and caught it. "Probably from Big Creek," he said, referring to a big logging operation several miles northeast of us, "they've got a big one going." He added that there were forest fires to the south of us in Oregon's Tillamook and Linn counties, and far to the north along the Washington coast.

"This is the damndest fall I ever seen, Sam," he sighed. "If we don't get rain soon this whole country'll be afire."

Forest fires were deadly, destructive, and frightening but during my boyhood years in a logging camp they were an accepted hazard. You lived with them the same as you lived with hurricanes, earthquakes, and floods. In my half-dozen years in a logging camp I had lived through double that number of fires. Most of them I was too young to remember.

But I remembered the dark, stifling days when Camp 2 burned and a dozen of Dave Tweedle's pigs were roasted on the hoof. Dad brought home a big chunk and we were pleased at first because fresh pork was a rare treat at the Western Cooperage camp.

Mother trimmed off the fire-blackened exterior and found the interior cooked to perfection. Then she started carefully slicing thick pieces as broad as the palm of Dad's hand onto a serving platter. Dad and I sat at the heavy oak, round, pedestal dining-room table that marked the dining area of our unpartitioned, one-room house. Dad was eying the mashed potatoes, gravy, homemade bread, and pickles Mother already had in place to go with the pork. Suddenly Mother laid down the bone-handled carving knife that was part of a wedding gift carving set and stood looking at the piece of pork.

"I can't do this," she said, turning to Dad and looking pale and sick. "I keep thinking of those poor pigs cooked alive." She just up and spoiled everything.

Dad nodded in understanding. "I was thinking the same thing," he admitted.

I hadn't been thinking of anything but eating some of that fresh pork. But now I didn't feel hungry, either.

Dad picked up the platter and started toward the door. "I'll take it over to Mrs. Johnson," he said. He returned in a few minutes, smiling, and carrying a kettle of beans. "I made a trade," he grinned, setting the kettle of beans on top of the cookstove. We all agreed that Mrs. Johnson couldn't cook beans as well as Mother. That night I dreamed of forest fires and burning pigs. The next day when I talked with Jake and Fen they said the roast pig was real good.

But there was a difference in the weather the day Camp 2 burned and this September day in 1918. This day was scary like. The men waiting to board the crew train huddled in little groups. They talked in low tones and kept looking at the sky. There wasn't any of the laughing and joshing and playful roughhousing that loggers heading out to the job usually indulged in.

After the train left I stood for a long time listening to its labored chatter as it fought its way with its long string of empty cars up the canyon. I heard it whistle for the gravel pit where Mr. Carlson and the steam shovel crew got off to load gravel cars for railroad ballast. I waited a little longer until I heard it whistle again. This time, I knew, it was whistling for Camp 2, almost three miles distant. From the Camp 2 spur it would follow the north line that crawled upward along the side of a timbered slope and finally doubled back along the east slope to the top of the ridge and Camp 7.

Camp 7 was a Spruce Division camp supervised by the Spruce Production Corporation set up by the War Department to log spruce timber used in airplanes. Millions of board feet of spruce from Pacific Northwest forests took to the air in World War I as wing frames and fuselages of Allied warplanes. There were about three hundred and fifty men at Camp 7, all of them in the Army. They had their rifles and ammunition with them at camp even though the nearest fighting trench was some seven thousand miles east in a land I knew only by name, France.

The railroad routes to Camp 2 and Camp 7 were as familiar as the underbrush path to our outdoor toilet; Mother and I had walked and ridden them many a time during summer and fall in search of wild blackberries and huckleberries for pies and jelly and canning.

With the crew train well on its way, I walked over and climbed up into the cab of the main-line engine that hauled the logs from our camp to the tidewater dump at Olney. The rumble of burning oil in the firebox drowned out normal conversation so I had to yell at engineer Jim Casey.

"Mr. Casey, I'm scared," I yelled.

"What are you scared of?" he yelled back motioning to

the fireman to ease up on the oil flow to the firebox so things would quiet down and we could talk.

"I'm scared that maybe something bad's going to happen today," I said. "Something real terrible bad. Maybe a fire."

He took a stick match from his overall pocket and scratched it against the wooden sill of the cab window. He blew on the flame of the lighted match but it wouldn't go out. It flared and fluttered like the flame on a stubborn birthday candle. "That's a bad sign," he said. He said when a match held its flame that way it meant the moisture content of the air was low. In such dry air a wood spark from a donkey engine would linger long. Possibly long enough to start a speck of fire in dry needles or twigs or other trash that lay in heaps around logging areas. In air so dry a steel cable rubbing against a tinder-dry stump or snag or windfall might start a fire just by friction.

After pointing out what could happen and why Mr. Casey set my mind partially at ease by adding that with fire spotters patrolling the woods area, and with men like Dad and Uncle Marsh watching over things, a fire was unlikely.

Mr. Casey pulled a silver-cased watch from a pocket in the bib of his overalls. He said it was time to go to work but that I could ride in the engine cab while they went for a trainload of logs parked on a storage siding above the camp. The little locomotive eased clear of the siding and on to the main line, then backed up to where the loaded cars of logs were waiting. Locomotives from the logging areas delivered cars of logs to the storage tracks and Mr. Casey's engine took them the rest of the way to Olney and the dumping grounds on Youngs River.

As the train was about to start its ten-mile trip to Olney I climbed down from the cab and stood well back from the tracks as the train began to move. The engine had rounded a curve and was out of sight before I noticed that burning oil which must have ignited from the locomotive's firebox had set fire to a crosstie between the rails. It seemed to get bigger and bigger as each loaded car passed over it. I was almost in a panic before the last car of the train came into sight and coasted by leaving the tracks clear. It wasn't a big fire but it was persistent as the flame on Mr. Casey's match. I stamped on it and beat it with damp marsh grass that grew in the mucky soil of a drain ditch next to the tracks. But the flame was stubborn and wouldn't go out. I was about to make a dash for the machine shop a few hundred feet beyond the curve and get help when I heard the click of wheels on rail joints. It was a section crew speeder (a small four-wheeled track car with a gasoline engine) with a fire guard. His job was to follow the log trains in summer and fall and put out fires that hot metal sparks from the car brakes could cause. He had a water barrel strapped to the speeder. He dipped out water with a can and poured it on the fire.

He had seen me trying to put out the fire. He shook his head and smiled at me. "There's fire in the sky today," he said. I looked up at the sky, startled. He laughed and said he didn't actually mean the sky was on fire. "She's a bad day. A fire day," he explained. "It's a fire in the sky day," he added, motioning toward the smoke haze and coppery color of the sun and sky.

I climbed aboard the speeder and rode down to our house. We put out four more track fires during the short ride. He asked if I wanted to ride with him to Olney and back. I could help him spot and put out fires. I wanted to go like anything. But I couldn't. I was now a first grader and it was a Thursday and in another hour I had to go to school.

It was not a comfortable day at school. A brisk wind from out of the east whistled down the canyon and through camp from midmorning on. It brought in more smoke and ashes and cinders from the Big Creek fire. The smoke build-up was so heavy that the sun almost disappeared from the sky and daylight in the school dwindled to where it was almost impossible to read. Even with the door at each end open it got awfully warm. Miss Della Brown, the teacher that year, dismissed classes early in the afternoon.

"If any of you have matches in your pockets give them to your mother as soon as you get home," she suggested. She was looking at Fen and Jake Johnson when she made the suggestion. She knew they both smoked and might be tempted to light up a roll-your-own Bull Durham on the way home. It wasn't a day for careless smoking.

By the time Dad and the other logger husbands came in on the crew train at the end of the day the wind, still from the east, was tugging at Mother's sweet peas planted between our house and the railroad track. It rattled through the underbrush and around the eaves of the house and connecting shake-sided woodshed.

Dad didn't talk much at supper. I told him about Mr. Casey and how he had tested the humidity by blowing on a lighted match. I told him about the burning tie and how I couldn't put it out. He nodded sort of absently as though he were listening but thinking about something else. I told him I was scared. That I bet we were going to have a fire and that maybe the camp would burn up. And that maybe we'd all be cooked alive like Mr. Tweedle's pigs when Camp 2 burned.

The thing that made me nervous was that he wasn't eating his pie. It was apple pie, and apple was Big Sam's favorite pie. I asked if he was scared and was that why he wasn't eating his pie? He said he was thinking about what I had been saying and that there was no need to be afraid. He said that in a logging camp and with such a brisk east wind there could be a fire. An east wind in the coastal forests of the West during summer and fall is a devil wind. Dad and the other men called it a fire wind. It was greedy and thirsty and would nose along the forest floor and in the brush and in logged-over areas snatching every bit of moisture it could find. You could always tell an east wind without knowing directions because an east wind was hot and dried up everything. Moss on the forest floor was usually moist and cool; after an east wind it was stiff and brittle. After a few hours in an east wind ferns would droop and pitch would well out through cracks in spruce trees the same as sweat on Dad's face when he was hard at work.

I again told Dad I was frightened and that the fire guard on the speeder had said today was a fire in the sky day. Dad said he had never heard a hot day called a fire in the sky day but it was just a name. If there would happen to be a fire, he said, it wouldn't be around the headquarters camp where we lived. It would be in the area of rebuilt Camp 2 or up around Camp 7 where the company was logging and where there had been a small fire a few days ago.

"We got that fire out, now didn't we?" he said. It was almost dark and near bedtime. He suggested I get undressed and crawl into bed. "They's nothing to worry about so you sleep good," he said. I got undressed and into my pajamas and Mother tucked me in. Dad got up from the table and went outside. I heard him strike a match and then blow on the flame just as Mr. Casey had done.

If there was nothing to worry about, I wondered, why was Dad blowing on a lighted match? And why was his apple pie still not eaten?

It seemed I had barely gotten to sleep when I was sitting bolt upright on the edge of my cot and wide awake. Jim Casey's locomotive was blowing its whistle like crazy, a long and a short, a long and a short repeated over and over. Every boy and girl in the Western Cooperage knew the meaning of that call. It meant fire. Mr. Irving was hammering on our front door and yelling for Dad. He was so wrought up his voice sounded almost as though he were sobbing. "Wake up, Sam," he was shouting. "Camp 7's going and the whole mountain's aflaming."

Dad's bare feet hit the floor with a thump. Seconds later I heard Mother's. She came over and pushed back the shade and peered out the window at the head of my cot. I rolled over on my stomach so I could get a look too. Neither of us was prepared for the sight that met our eyes. The entire night sky to the northeast in the direction of Camp 7 was a whirling inferno of ugly orange. It was as though the very forces of hell itself had burst free of the earth and were attacking the heavens. Maelstroms of flame seemed to leap free of the main fire and hurtle off like flares into space. A storm of ash, cinders, and half-burned pieces of limb tips and twigs whirled by the window, pushed by the wind.

When Dad opened the door for a better look, the sounds of the fire, a rumbling roar, filled the room. "It sounds loud and looks close but it's five or six miles away," Dad said. By now men were running up the railroad track past our house toward the glaring headlights and clanking sounds of locomotives hooking onto crew cars. Dad gave Mother and me a hurried kiss, a word or two of reassurance, and hurried to join the others.

"When will you be home?" Mother called out after him as he disappeared in the darkness toward the waiting locomotives. We waited but there was no answer. "I guess he didn't hear me," Mother said, more to herself than to me. Suddenly the little house seemed terrifyingly big and frightfully lonely. I began to cry. Mother dropped to her knees beside my cot. She put an arm around me and drew me close. "It's a terrible fire but don't be frightened," she whispered. "Your father and the other men will be there soon and then everything will be all right." I had a feeling she didn't feel as optimistic as she tried to sound but before I had a chance to do any more worrying Mrs. Johnson's familiar voice boomed into the room.

"You and little Samuel all right?" she asked, poking her head through the open doorway. Dad hadn't closed the door when he left. Mother's voice sounded ten years younger when she answered. "Come in, come in," she said. Mrs. Johnson came on in. She was dressed in one of Mr. Johnson's nightgowns and slippers and had her corncob pipe between her teeth. She looked as unconcerned as though she had just gotten up to go to the toilet. "All hell's running loose tonight," she muttered, looking back out the open doorway in the direction of the fire.

Mother stared at her in wonder and undisguised affection. Her lower lip began to quiver. In the yellow glow of the lamp on the dining table I could see the glisten of tears starting to well up in her eyes. Suddenly the tensions of the past half-hour broke loose. She put her arms around Mrs. Johnson and began to cry in great heaving sobs that shook her whole body from hairnet to toes.

Mrs. Johnson looked over Mother's shoulder at me. "Now why don't you get under the covers and go to sleep and let us women have a good cry?" she suggested.

"Are you going to cry, too?" I asked.

"I don't want no little boy looking at me if I do," she answered.

I didn't know what time it was but I guessed it must be near midnight. I had no doubt that no matter what happened from now on Mrs. Johnson could handle it. All of a sudden I just couldn't help myself. I jumped out of bed, asked Mrs. Johnson to bend down, and gave her a great big kiss right next to her pipe stem and square on the mouth. I hopped back in bed and was under the covers before she issued her startled, "Jumpin' devils and hollerin' hell. What's that for?"

"I love you," I said.

I must have started fading off into sleep almost immediately because I could hear Mrs. Johnson muttering to Mother and her voice sounded as though she were way off in the distance. She was saying something like "If you've got a little whiskey about, Caroline," she said, "it's time we both had a couple of good snorts."

The forest fire didn't look half as dangerous the next morning but that was only because the angry glow that had filled the sky during the night faded from sight in the daylight. Smoke filled the canyon and blanketed the camp in suffocating layers that completely blocked out the sun. Mother did her housework by lamplight. Ash and other fire debris drifted over everything. When I went outside to get a bucket of water for Mother the layer of ashes and cinders was deep enough so that I left a trail of footprints exactly as though I were walking in snow. The odor of scorched timber was everywhere and the dense smoke stung your eyes and throat and made breathing difficult.

The fire had wiped out several spur lines and Camp 7 was gone. Jim Irving returned from the fire lines briefly about midmorning. He told Mother not to worry, that Dad and the other men were bone-weary but safe. He said when the fire hit Camp 7 it set off hundreds of rounds of ammunition and lead and shell jackets were whizzing around until fighting the fire was not much different from being on a battle line. In its wild sweep of the previous night the fire had blackened several thousand acres of logged-over land and left four donkey engines smoking, twisted burned-out hulks.

Although the heavy blanket of smoke turned day almost into night and made it impossible to get a visual appraisal of the fire's progress, a steady firing of dynamite blasts told us that the fire hadn't been satisfied with its battle score of four donkey engines and all of Camp 7. It was roaring toward the forward wall of virgin forest that stood between it and us. The men were using dynamite in an effort to blast out trees and snags in hopes of establishing partially cleared paths or fire lines that would slow the fire's advance.

By the time I left for school the roaring crackle of the flames was plainly audible. Winds surged at cross-purposes up and down and back and forth across the canyon as the monstrous drafts generated by the fire clashed with the steady east wind that was flooding the camp with deluges of smoke, ash, and sometimes burning sections of limb.

Advance of the fire toward the headquarters camp had been anticipated because sometime during the night or early morning Jim Irving had stationed a half-dozen or so men from the railroad section crew at strategic locations to spot burning debris and put it out. A couple of men were on the machine shop and cookhouse roofs. Others kept an eye on the bunkhouse and family houses. They carried water-soaked gunny sacks with which to beat out spot fires started by the hot brands and ashes.

The fire was still some three miles from camp when school was dismissed and we were told to go home immediately. During the hour or so we had been in school the smoke had gotten much worse. The east wind had increased and was funneling smoke and blistering hot ashes into the canyon and over the camp. Flecks of ashes that during the night piled up like snow now rushed in like a blizzard.

Racing from school to the crossing and up the railroad track as fast as I could go, I noticed that there were more men with gunny sacks slapping out spot fires. And in front of our house a locomotive with a string of empty cars sat, waiting. It was Mr. Casey's. I rushed into the house. The roar of the fire suddenly sounded like a thousand freight trains. Giant fir and hemlock, burst apart by the terrific heat, exploded and crashed to earth with ground-shaking roars. I let out a wail of terror. "We're going to die," I screamed in panic at Mother.

She was sitting at the dining table. It was not yet noon and a kerosene lamp was burning. A man sat across the table from her wolfing down meat, homemade bread and jelly, and water by the quart. His eyebrows and hair were singed. His face and arms and hands were black from fire grime. He offered me a hand. It was blistered and scarred. I ignored the hand and rushed instead to Mother. I peered across the table at him. It was minutes before the truth dawned on me. This caricature in black was Dad.

Even as I watched him, he pushed the empty plate from in front of him, rested his arms and head on the table, and within seconds was snoring.

Mother tapped her lips with a forefinger. "Your father's

exhausted," she whispered. "Let's be real quiet and let him sleep."

While Dad slept, Mother and I tiptoed outside and climbed into the cab of Mr. Casey's locomotive. It was his locomotive that had brought Dad and some of the others to camp for food and a short rest. Most of the men were being fed from Camp 2, Mr. Casey said. He said Dad and the other men would probably be called back in an hour. The fire had slowed a little when it hit the green timber and if it could be stopped before it reached the camp it would be now. The only thing that had saved the camp so far was that the fire for some reason or other was staying on the ground. It hadn't crowned, lifted to the tops of the trees and raced from top to top. If it did that it could wipe out the camp in less than an hour's time. Because of that danger Mr. Irving had ordered Mr. Casey's locomotive with several flat cars to stand by at the camp in case we had to evacuate.

There was one hope, said Mr. Casey. Up on the mountain above the smoke and low-level curtain of ash, it was clear enough to see a curtain of fog and some rain clouds moving in from the southwest.

"A drippy fog or rain might save us," he said.

"If you don't mind my saying so," said Mother, "I think we ought to ask God to hurry the fog."

"If we're going to ask for something let's ask for a helluva lot of rain," said Mr. Casey.

Mother nodded in agreement. I wasn't sure whether Mr. Casey was serious or kidding, but Mother seemed to think he meant what he said. She and I climbed down from the cab and went around back of our house where Dad had his vegetable garden.

"I think you should pray, too," said Mother, kneeling down on the bare earth where earlier in the season Dad had grown big heads of lettuce.

Ever after, Mother referred to Dad's garden as our prayer garden. It was a comfortable place in which to pray, I guess because it was secluded and people couldn't peek in on you as though curious about what God and you were talking about.

I wasn't sure that God could do much about stopping the fire since Big Sam and the other loggers weren't having much luck. But I did tell Him that Uncle Marsh would be madder than a cougar cat if God let his house burn up.

Mother had quite a bit to say so she hadn't finished by the time I had. I felt guilty, kneeling there beside her and listening to what she and God were saying. But it didn't seem proper to get up and walk away during a prayer. It might hurt God's feelings or make Him think you didn't like Him. So there was nothing I could do but continue kneeling and listening.

I thought Mother gave God a lot of things to think about. She said she wasn't questioning His reasons but if He let our camp burn He would be hurting a lot of fine people. She admitted they had faults. They swore a lot, even to taking His name in vain; they drank and sometimes got out of hand and noisy; and they hadn't been very nice to Mr. Michelson when he tried to start a Sunday school. But she listed a lot of their good qualities such as Mrs. Johnson coming over last night to see how Mother and I were, and how Mrs. Lillich and Mrs. Kneeland and other women at the old camp helped Mother when she was a newlywed and I was a baby. She said a lot of other nice things about the camp and its people and I would have bet my brand new Daisy air rifle against one of Fen Johnson's skunk hides that God was listening.

By the time we got back in the house Dad had awakened. He was peeling his underwear down to the waist in readiness for a brisk upper-body and face and hands scrubbing. He was almost as black underneath as he was on top. He scrubbed outside with lye soap and cold water straight out of the supply pipe next to the front porch. It was the nearest thing we had to inside plumbing. After several minutes with soap and

water, and with help from Mother, he began to look like
Dad. Next he took off his calk shoes and wool socks. He
rolled up the legs of his long underwear and scrubbed his feet
and legs. Looking refreshed, he went inside the house and
scrubbed the middle part of his body with a wet cloth. Mother
outfitted him with a clean change of clothes, poured him a
pint dipper of black coffee, and he was ready for another
twelve hours on the fire line.

Another locomotive was waiting to take Dad and the
others who had been given two or three hours off to eat and
rest up back up on the hill to the fire. As Dad was leaving the
house he sniffed the air and cocked a trained ear toward the
fire.

"You better pack a few things in case we have to make a
run for it," he advised Mother. But he said it sounded to him
as though the fire had quieted a little. "Feel that bit of cool
breeze?" he asked. "By jingo there's the smell of rain in the
air."

"We prayed and it's gonna rain," I shouted at Mr. Casey.

"Remember this day and the goodness of God," Mother
directed.

To be honest I couldn't see that it was any cooler and I
couldn't smell anything with the odor of rain, but with both
Dad and God fighting for us and the camp I was no longer
frightened and I suddenly was terribly sleepy and in need of
a nap.

To be on the safe side Mother did as Dad had directed. She
began putting a few family possessions in a trunk. "If we
have to go with Mr. Casey's train," she warned me, "we can
take only a few things." She suggested I pick out one or two
of my possessions. The rest would have to remain behind if
we were evacuated. I had a treasure box of stuff buried at
the base of an old stump near the house, but I doubted
Mother would let me take it. It didn't contain anything of
real value but there were items of great sentimental worth.
There was a kinky string of metal shaving cut from a piece of

steel by the big turning lathe in the machine shop. There were some old nuts and bolts and a bit of coal from the blacksmith shop, a railroad spike, a smashed steam gage off a yarding donkey, and a pair of work gloves Dad had worn out and thrown away.

There were two things I knew I must take—my Teddy bear and my new Daisy air rifle. The Teddy bear had slept with me every night of my life for as long as I could remember.

I watched to see what Mother was taking. She was awfully slow in deciding. There were clothes for Dad and me, a dress for her that she said was her wedding dress, a Bible her mother had given her, a picture of Dad and her when they were married, my baby shoes which seemed silly since I couldn't wear them any more, a Bucksport, Maine, cookbook, and a long-stemmed goblet which she carefully wrapped in fold after fold of newspaper.

We didn't have much but after the trunk was filled it seemed we were leaving behind an awful lot. With a startled little cry, Mother rushed to the dresser. From a drawer she removed her wedding book and my baby book. "How could I have overlooked these for even a moment," she chided herself.

One moment it was hot and stuffy and I was sitting in my rocking chair watching Mother pack. The next thing I knew it was night and Dad and Mother were sitting at the table talking in low tones by lamplight. The side and front door of the house was open and a cool breeze was whipping through. And I was in bed. And rain was clumping down on our tarpaper roof.

I bounded out of bed and ran to look out the side door. "God did it!" I yelled in a voice that was a mixture of awe and excitement. "God did it because He's ascared of Uncle Marsh."

My noisy exit from the bed bounced both Mother and Dad out of their chairs. I stood in the open doorway, clad in pajamas, breathing full measures of the fresh, cool air, and tingling with relief and pleasure as soft fingers of rain brushed against my face and hair.

Mother and Dad came over and stood beside me. The glow of the fire still looked down on the camp from the northeastern sky but it was not the lunging, billowing thing of terror it had been the previous night. The terrible monster of a few hours ago was dying and our camp home was safe.

Mother wanted to know what I meant when I said God was afraid of Uncle Marsh. I told her of my prayer. How I had warned God that Uncle Marsh would be madder than a cougar cat if God let Uncle Marsh's house burn.

"Even God wouldn't want to fight Uncle Marsh," I said.

"God was kind to us because He loves us, not because He was afraid of us," said Mother. "Always remember, God is your friend."

I knew in my heart that Mother was right. But I knew, too, that Mother's and my prayers had been answered. Probably God had listened more to Mother because she was older and nearer His age. But it seemed logical to me to assume that when He sent the rain He had Uncle Marsh in mind, too.

26. This now peaceful log dump once handled as many as three trainloads of logs each day. Almost one billion feet of virgin timber were rafted and towed from this dump.

27. The logging crew at Tidewater Timber Company's summit camp. Uncle Marshall, wearing a sweater and holding his hat, is sixth from the right in the front row. *(Photo courtesy of Ball Studio, Astoria, Oregon)*

28. This is logger country—as it appeared in 1955. Now it is covered with planted forest.

29. Tillamook Burn in Oregon's Tillamook County. The white snags on the ridge are ghostly monuments to forest fires that ravaged the area. It is now being reforested.

30. Big fir stumps are today half hidden by second generation hemlock growth. Big Sam very likely worked at this very spot.

31. Only memories remain. Young Sam stands on the rotted, sagging floor of what was once the bunkhouse he shared with Big Sam while working as a logger.

32. The stump of The Big Tree.

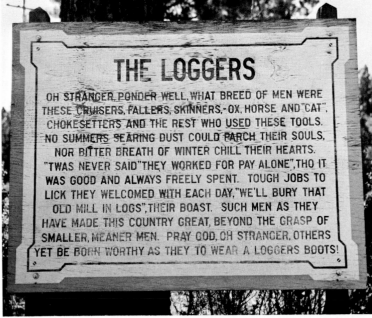

## THE LOGGERS

OH STRANGER PONDER WELL, WHAT BREED OF MEN WERE
THESE CRUISERS, FALLERS, SKINNERS,-OX, HORSE AND "CAT",
CHOKESETTERS AND THE REST WHO USED THESE TOOLS.
NO SUMMERS SEARING DUST COULD PARCH THEIR SOULS,
NOR BITTER BREATH OF WINTER CHILL THEIR HEARTS.
"TWAS NEVER SAID "THEY WORKED FOR PAY ALONE", THO IT
WAS GOOD AND ALWAYS FREELY SPENT. TOUGH JOBS TO
LICK THEY WELCOMED WITH EACH DAY, "WE'LL BURY THAT
OLD MILL IN LOGS", THEIR BOAST. SUCH MEN AS THEY
HAVE MADE THIS COUNTRY GREAT, BEYOND THE GRASP OF
SMALLER, MEANER MEN. PRAY GOD, OH STRANGER, OTHERS
YET BE BORN WORTHY AS THEY TO WEAR A LOGGERS BOOTS!

33. The sign at Collier Memorial Park and Logging Museum on U.S. Highway 97 some thirty-three miles north of Klamath Falls, Oregon. "Chokesetters" should actually be "choker setters," the choker being the steel cable with sliding hook that was attached over the end of a log to be dragged in by donkey engine. The ode was written by Nelson Reed.

## Chapter 13

## WHISTLE WHILE YOU WORK

In the Western Cooperage camp life was regimented by whistles. When Mrs. Johnson wanted Fen or Jake she placed her thumb and index finger against her lower lip and tongue. Then she'd exhale a blast of air. The combination produced an earsplitting screech that would carry a mile or more.

Whistling was an accomplishment Mother never mastered. In fact it didn't seem to run in our family. Dad was no good at it and I could barely produce enough sound to carry a tune. Even though Mother couldn't whistle worth a darn she didn't have to take a back seat to any mother in the camp. When she'd stand on our front porch and yell out, "Saaaaaaa-amm yooooooooool," it covered most of the nearby areas. I heard her once when I was at the Fischer and Leitzel camp and that was almost a mile away.

A stream of short blasts from the little Climax locomotive at Fischer and Leitzel would send all eight grades at the Western Cooperage school rushing to the south windows. The warning cry meant the little engine was out of control on the company's steep railroad grade and a wreck with flying logs and torn-up track was possibly minutes away.

Sometimes after such a mishap the Fischer and Leitzel camp would be quiet for days while the engine crew got the battered little veteran back in operating condition. The ingenuity and patience exhibited by the average logger in such situations never ceased to amaze Mother. She could never fathom how men, many of whom, like Dad, could barely read, could do such incredible things as build railroad trestles,

repair smashed and broken equipment including locomotives
and donkey engines, lay out camp sites and railroad lines.

To her way of thinking each of these accomplishments demanded a certain amount of education and great amounts of
native ability and skill. In Boston a plumber was a plumber, a
carpenter a carpenter, a construction engineer a highly
trained individual. Each excelled in some one thing and knew
very little about any other line of work.

At the Western Cooperage camp and in every logging
camp from British Columbia to California each worker
seemed to come equipped with a dozen skills. A hooktender
could run donkey or take the throttle of a locomotive if he
had to. Uncle Marsh could build a house, lay out a rough
course for a railroad, or look at a block of timber and know
immediately where to place a half-dozen or so donkey engines to log it most efficiently.

Dad, a man who suffered agonies and would sweat as
though involved in hard labor whenever he had to write his
name, could watch a straining main-line cable stretched tight
as a bow string between a power-crazed donkey engine and
twenty tons of stubborn log, and know almost to the pound
when the line had reached the breaking point.

Mother was never hesitant in telling T. W. Robinson, the
camp superintendent, that men with such diversity of talent
and ability were entitled to more out of life than four dollars a day wages and the humiliation of being ordered around
by a steam whistle.

"Oh, for heaven's sakes, Caroline," was Mr. Robinson's
usual answer. If Dad happened to be handy, Mr. Robinson
would turn to him in feigned exasperation. "Sam, why
couldn't you have married some quiet, reasonable girl from
Astoria?" But he was an admirer of Mother's.

"You do what your mother tells you," he often told me,
"and you'll amount to something." That was almost like a
command direct from Heaven, coming as it did from Mr.
Robinson. There wasn't much I could say but "Yes, sir."

No matter what Mother contended in those early days, loggers have remained loggers and most of their working days continue to be dominated by whistles—electric these days, instead of steam.

Although all whistles may have sounded alike to a newcomer in camp they were as individualistic as night and day to us. The possibility of confusing the whistle call of a yarding donkey on Side One with that of a road donkey on Side Two was as remote as mistaking the voices of Mother and Mrs. Johnson. There wasn't an individual in camp, adult or youngster, who couldn't give you an instant status report on the day's logging operations from the constant chatter of steam donkey whistles.

Monitoring the whistle calls was a subconscious process. You were rarely aware that your mind was checking off each signal as it floated in from the logging areas. But it was. Throughout the working day the movement of every log from cutting area to railroad spur line where it was loaded onto rail cars was guided by shouted commands which were relayed to the distant donkey engine operator by triggering a steam whistle mounted on the engine's boiler. The triggering was done by a "whistle punk" jerking a wire stretched through the woods and leading from the work area to the donkey engine. Whistle punks were usually young fellows in their teens and "punking" or blowing whistle was the starting job in the woods. A whistle punk had to know some two dozen signal combinations and a dozen special calls in relaying shouted calls of the rigging crew to the donkey engineer. Each need—go ahead on the main line, slack the haulback, stop all lines, call the foreman—had its special call. Later, when giant multiengined machines mounted on rail cars and called skidders were in action, a whistle punk had to know dozens of complex signal combinations and his hand and reflexes controlled tons of lethal rigging both on the ground and overhead.

Sitting in the Western Cooperage school and trying to con-

centrate on arithmetic or geography while the shouts of a
half-dozen donkey engine whistles yammered at you was
often a problem. Mastery of the multiplication tables sometimes couldn't compete with a yarder having a tough time
dragging in an oversized log that might weigh as much as
thirty tons. Logs hung up on stumps or other obstacles on
their way to the donkey engine would often send a whistle
into a screaming tirade as the rigging crew worked to free
the log and send it on its way.

Mother contended at such times that it was just as though
the whistle were swearing. In the daily fury of logging it
often seemed that the whistles of the various donkey engines
were shouting to each other.

There was nothing pleasant or relaxing about the sound of
a steam donkey whistle. It always sounded impatient,
angry, and militant. It never requested; it ordered. High-
pitched and nagging, it was no respecter of job rank or authority. It treated everyone exactly alike. When Mr. Irving
was needed, a whistle would summon him with four long
blasts repeated at intervals. If he didn't get there right away
and the whistle kept calling, Mother and other wives in the
camp might make comments such as: "I wonder where Mr.
Irving is? Why doesn't he answer his call?"

Over the years a whistle signal had evolved for just about
everything imaginable. Three short blasts in series of three
meant the donkey engine was low on fuel and to hook on a
waste log that could be dragged in and cut into long slabs
for the firebox. Two long was a message to the man tending
the gasoline water pump located at some nearby creek or
spring dammed to form a pond; it meant start the pump
and send us water. When the donkey engine's water tank
was full, a long blast from the whistle meant to stop pumping
water.

A long blast followed by a short one started the crews to
work in the morning and announced quitting time at the end
of the day. Three long bursts, repeated at intervals, was the

loggers' way of requesting a locomotive to switch out loaded cars and bring in empty ones.

Out where choker setters were hooking the main-line rigging onto the ends of logs so that the donkey engine could drag them in, the whistle not only controlled log movement—it often regulated life and death. A wrong or misinterpreted whistle call might send writhing tons of rigging hurtling into a man. A big road donkey might drag logs for almost a mile. Once on the job the donkey engineer and the rigging crew might not see each other the rest of the day until the final whistle and quitting time; during this ten-hour interval the only line of communication was the thin stranded wire (similar to a backyard clothesline) that ran from the donkey engine whistle to the whistle punk.

Donkey engine whistles were the gossips. They couldn't keep a secret and they weren't meant to. Day after day they screeched, pouted, harassed, and assailed the ears and nerves of man and beast from the surf line of the Pacific to the snow line of the Cascade Range.

They had an entirely different personality in the middle of the night. Sometimes a tumbling sapling or a heavy limb would fall across the whistle wire at night. The weight of the intruder would absorb the slack and cause the wire to trip the donkey whistle. A whistle so tripped would send out a dead-of-the-night call eerie and ghostly enough to make your flesh crawl. Each logging side, or unit, had a night watchman. He made his rounds of the great resting engines, seeing that the wood fires were banked so there would be steam in the boilers when the crews reported for work in the morning. It was a lonely, scary job, tramping from donkey engine to donkey engine through the woods by lantern light all night long.

Whenever a donkey whistle was accidentally tripped in the middle of the night it would blow until the watchman could reach it and locate the trouble or disconnect the whistle wire.

Sometimes it would be almost an hour before the whistle could be quieted and peace and quiet restored.

Even Dad, who seemed to fear nothing and could sleep through most any calamity including cougar calls, windstorms, and I think even earthquakes, would wake up with nerves on edge when a night whistle sounded. "When's that watchman going to shut that thing off?" he'd snap irritably. Thinking of the watchman hurrying through the woods, surrounded by a tiny circle of kerosene lantern light in a forest of blackness, unnerved Mother more than the ghostly sound of the whistle.

"I wouldn't be out there alone for all the tea in Boston," she'd announce, snuggling up in a ball against Dad's back. The eerie call of a night whistle usually sent me scampering under the covers with Mother and Dad. Our cat, Muff, often made it a foursome.

"Git that cat out of this bed," Dad would roar. "Hush up and go to sleep," Mother would whisper, her voice muffled by the covers pulled up over her head.

Day or night the tone of a locomotive whistle was pleasing and implanted with warmth, friendliness, and indulgence. It was just as authoritative as a steam donkey whistle but it handled itself better.

"Whistles are no different than people," Mother used to point out. "Just remember, a whisper is often louder than a shout."

The throaty warning call of a logging locomotive as it neared the camp with a long train of loaded log cars would send us youngsters scampering for vantage points to watch its clattering passage through camp. The goings and comings of trains seemed to be of great interest to everyone. Housewives would stop their housework, cooking, or washing to step to the doorway and wave to the train crew. The office, cookhouse and shop crews always seemed to have a few spare minutes in which to watch. For the men this casual work stoppage two or three times a day was prompted by more than idle curiosity and interest in locomotives and log-ging-railroad rolling stock. The log trains provided a clue as to how things were going at the logging end. Short trains of fifteen or twenty cars meant the donkey engines and their crews were in exceptionally rough country, or having break-downs or other problems, that slowed production. On the other hand, long trains of twenty-five to thirty or thirty-five cars meant things were highballing, going full blast.

Passage of the log trains revealed the quality of timber coming out of the woods. Car after car of giant Douglas fir logs, fifty-two feet in length or even more, and of uniform size and yellowish in color, indicated highest quality, top price from mills and no interruption of pay checks.

Although it was God's forest Big Sam and the others were logging, each man on a logging camp crew took a personal pride in it. If the timber quality was poor the men often reacted as though in some way it was their fault. They tended to blame themselves as though they had failed somewhere along the way and were now being repaid with an inferior product.

Most of the whistle signals that bombarded the Western Cooperage camp were routine in nature and had to do with the day-in, day-out business of logging. But there were two that would immediately put our or any camp on edge. One was the repetition of long and short blasts which meant fire. The other, more feared than a dozen fires and affecting every household, was seven long followed by two short and re-peated over and over. This signified, "Man injured. Send a stretcher."

A whistle call for a stretcher meant serious injury in a logging camp. Minor injuries such as broken arms, cracked ribs, broken jaws rarely interrupted the throb of the big yard-ing, road donkey, and loading engines. As long as a man was conscious and able to walk he usually made his own way to the railroad loading site. If a locomotive or speeder was on its way to camp he might hitch a ride. If not, he would walk the distance and think nothing of it.

When a man was hurt badly enough to require a stretcher he had to have at least a broken leg, smashed foot, skull injury, or crushed rib cage. In other words, he was so badly hurt he would have to be carried out.

Whenever the "dead whistle," as we youngsters called it, sounded the womenfolk of the camp would gather in little groups on the railroad track in front of their homes. They talked in low tones and kept close watch in the direction of the office. The goings and comings of camp officials such as T. W. Robinson or Jim Irving might suggest a clue.

There were other sounds worth paying attention to. The big machines in an area where a man had been seriously hurt would take their ease on their big wooden sleds while crews were bringing him out. It would take most of a crew to man a stretcher in the jumble of downed timber, logs, brush, and logging debris that cluttered a logging area.

If the machines resumed their work you knew the injured man had been removed to the safety of the railroad spur that served that particular logging unit and would soon be transported to camp by locomotive or speeder. If the great machines remained silent you knew the worst had happened—somebody's husband or father wouldn't be on the crew train when it rolled into camp at the end of the day. He wouldn't be on it ever again. It frightened you and made you sick inside. During those horrible, suspenseful periods of waiting, everyone looked at each other, hoping desperately and selfishly that God in His great wisdom and compassion had spared your loved one.

During these fearful moments I often found myself wondering in agony what life without Big Sam would be like. I suppose the same painful thought was in the mind of every boy and girl whose father worked in the ever present shadow of death or injury cast by the thunder-voiced machines.

To me there just couldn't be a Western Cooperage camp with no Big Sam shouting and sweating and leaping from log to log and crashing through brush, or stamping down the railroad track from the crew train at the end of the day, as big as two ordinary men, swinging his empty lunch bucket and with love for me and Mother poking out of his eyes when he'd meet up with us.

On one such wait I tugged at Mother's hand and asked why we didn't go to our prayer garden, the way we did during the Camp 7 fire, and ask God to make it be somebody else, not Dad. She squeezed my hand until it hurt. We went behind the house to the garden but when we got there Mother didn't kneel and pray as she had during the fire. Instead she sat me on a block sawed from the end of a log. Dad sometimes used it for a chopping block for cutting wood and kindling.

Squatting down to where we could look each other square in the face, she explained that it wouldn't be right to ask God to spare you and hurt somebody else. These were times, she said, "When we put our full trust in God." I tried desperately to keep faith with God and do as Mother said. But I just couldn't. Every time the "dead whistle" would blow, I'd close my eyes and murmur a hasty, silent plea, "Please God, don't let it be Dad."

Most of the time when the locomotive or speeder arrived at camp the injured man would be in pain and misery, but alive. Usually after a brief stop the engine or speeder would hurry right on down to Olney where an ambulance would be waiting to take him by road to the hospital in Astoria.

But there were times when the figure on the flat car or speeder's deck would be motionless and covered from head to foot by a blanket. Then Mr. Robinson or Mr. Irving, or maybe both, would walk toward the group of waiting women. There is no reasonable way in which to tell a wife that her husband is dead. But Mr. Robinson and Mr. Irving did their best to ease the shock and pain.

The other camp women did what they could to comfort and help. Each knew that the others might be comforting her the next time the "dead whistle" blew.

## Chapter 14

## THE LONG WALK

One day while overturning rocks in search of crawfish along Klaskanine Creek it suddenly struck me that the woods and camp area were uncommonly quiet. The tumbling creek waters were as chatty as usual. A midmorning breeze rustled and sniffed among the alders and salmonberry bushes that grew lush as a jungle along the creek banks. From the direction of the camp came the mighty thumps of the massive steam hammer in the blacksmith shop and the ring of hand hammers on metal. These were the usual sounds in a logging camp, but there was something missing. I couldn't put my finger on it but there was a sound, as familiar as the song of the creek, that was no longer present.

Throughout the morning of crawfish-hunting the identity of the missing sound escaped and troubled me. When I returned home Mother was frying doughnuts. A big iron skillet, heavy as a timber faller's ax, was half filled with hot grease on top of the wood-burning cookstove. Each time Mother dropped a ring of dough into the hot oil it bubbled and sizzled in a fit of temper, then settled down to the job of cooking. Nobody in camp could match Mother when it came to making doughnuts.

"You mightn't know much about cooking b'ar and deer meat, Caroline," Mrs. Johnson often told her, "but you got a way with doughnuts."

Munching on one doughnut and with a spare ringing a forefinger, I mentioned the unusual quiet to Mother. Always attentive to my questions, she interrupted her cooking chores long enough to step outside and listen. When she returned she looked a little perplexed, but she had the answer.

"There are no donkey engine whistles blowing," she explained. The Fischer and Leitzel camp had finished logging the ridge southwest of our camp several months previous and had moved away. Some of the old camp buildings, flimsy and not worth moving, had been left behind. But the railroad, donkey engines, and little Climax locomotive were gone. We had missed their sounds for a time but that was the story of logging—noise, activity and people in an area today; silence, emptiness, and loneliness tomorrow when the timber was gone.

The mystery of why we no longer heard the whistles of Western Cooperage donkey engines was cleared up by Dad when he came home from work that night. The big machines had moved south of Camp 2 and were now behind a ridge that choked off the sounds that for years had been a part of camp life. Those in the area of old Camp 7 were far back in the timber and now on a sidehill within sight of Big Creek donkey engines logging the opposite side of a separating canyon.

"The day will come when the donkey engines will meet and there won't be any more timber," Mother predicted, half serious and half in jest. Dad smiled. Mother's comment tickled me, too. There was no imagining the Western Cooperage and Clatsop County ever being without timber. To the southeast of us toward the summit of the low range of hills between us and Jewell there was ridge after ridge of primeval forest that had yet to hear the sound of a human voice. There were endless thousands of acres of sawlog timber where a man couldn't find a single mark made by ax or saw and he could spend the rest of his life looking.

Ours was a massive belt of timber encompassing virgin stands along the Lewis and Clark, Klaskanine, Walluski, and Youngs rivers. There were others, equally large, reaching back from the Columbia River along the John Day River and east into the Mary's Creek and Bear Creek drainage regions; and south from the Columbia along Big Creek and its tributaries. The Nehalem and Necanicum river basins were packed with timber. It seemed unlikely that man, with his cumbersome sled-mounted chargers would ever reach the end of this green bonanza were he to log day and night for a dozen lifetimes.

But Mother was never so certain of this as Dad and the others in the camp. She never hit upon the concept that now governs the timber industry—that timber is a renewable crop —but she came close in arguing with Dad that a forest was similar to a garden. "You plant in the spring so that we'll have fresh vegetables in the summer and early fall," she used to tell Dad.

Dad often appeared downright disgusted with her during some of these discussions. "Good Lord, Carrie," he'd snort, "it takes three months to grow a head of lettuce and a hundred years to grow a fir or hemlock. You and me ain't going to be around."

"I'm not thinking of us," Mother would answer. She said she was worried about me and my generation and following generations. Was it right for one generation to lay claim to, and use up, a natural resource that God quite possibly intended for all generations?

"I don't know what God intended," Dad would shrug. Sometimes Uncle Marsh would happen by during one of these family talks (topical discussions, Mother called them). "You give the order, Caroline," he'd say with a playful wink at Dad, "and we'll quit logging and plant trees." He'd tilt his chair back against the wall on two legs, slap his thighs with both hands, and shake the house with his laughter.

"Someday you may just do that," Mother would insist. Dad admired Mother and respected her ideas but the thought of logger crews turning farmers and planting a crop that wouldn't be ready to harvest for at least eighty years seemed so absurd that even he'd shake his head at Mother and smile.

One day I suggested to Mother that we pack a lunch and hike up to the logging area and watch the crews of men and machines at work. "It's a long walk," she said thoughtfully, "since the machines have moved." We decided to hike to Camp 2 instead. It was only three miles to Camp 2 but it took us the better part of three hours. Walking with Mother was always leisurely and fun. She enjoyed stopping and looking at things of interest along the way—trout in a pool, or a woodpecker thumping an old snag, or maybe a bear ambling across the tracks up ahead.

Camp 2 wasn't quite as I remembered it. The big, barnlike cookhouse and dining room were the same, as was the cluster of bunkhouses on the uphill side of the tracks. But there were some unexpected changes. The slope and high ridge across the creek from the camp, once all forest, was now a sun-blistered jungle of stumps, snags, and mangled brush with here and there a forlorn cluster of trees. It reminded me of illustrations of battlefields I had seen in the Portland *Oregonian* and *Oregon Journal* during World War I. It looked as though the big guns of war had been here and the forest had just up and run off, leaving its stumps and a few stragglers behind.

My favorite stump, alongside the railroad and near the cookhouse, from which I had often watched the big machines at work and even picked out Dad skittering along the length of a log, was anchored in the same old place but Dad and the machines had moved on and were no longer in sight. And the camp was so silent I could hear the burbles of Klaskanine Creek as it tumbled over rocks and logging debris at the bottom of the cayon. Across the canyon a locomotive with several loaded log cars felt its way along the branch line that wound through cuts and over trestles along the slope of the ridge and over the top to Camp 7.

For the first time I had an inkling of what Mother meant when she'd suggest to Dad that maybe the forest around us wouldn't be here forever. It still seemed incredible that a whole world of trees could be swallowed up as Mother said, but the bleakness that now surrounded Camp 2 made a person wonder.

On the way back to the headquarters camp where we lived I asked Mother what God would do with the land now that Dad and the others had finished with it. She said He probably would replant it to trees but that it probably would take mine and another lifetime before it would be even near what it was when men like Dad and Uncle Marsh first found it. She hurried on to explain that Dad and Uncle Marsh weren't doing anything wrong; that God had made Oregon so that He would have a garden in which to plant trees, and that He intended that man should cut and use the trees; but that man had not yet learned to utilize the forest as God intended. She wasn't certain in her own mind just how God might have wanted man to harvest it but she was certain He hadn't wanted man to waste and destroy it.

To my way of thinking God hadn't been as thorough in His planning as He might have been. In the nightmarish jumble of chopped-up land that was the Coast Range there was no easy, efficient method yet devised to log marketable timber without hurting the young and immature saplings. Heavy, powerful machines and intricate logging systems had to be developed to bring the logs from hogback, ridge, and canyon floor to railroad loading site. Where the railroad couldn't go, the yarders, road, and swing donkeys climbed, slashed, and pulled themselves on their monstrous sleds. They passed the logs from one to another, like a bucket brigade at a fire, bridging the torturous gap from cutting area to railroad cars at the loading site.

It was mean, brutal, and savage, taxing the strength and stamina of both men and machines. It sent a man tumbling into bed at the end of the day scarred, bruised, and exhausted. It made my mother determined that, "You aren't going to be a logger."

The logger of two generations ago had other problems.

Time, taxes, and fire dogged his every step. If he tarried one of the three would trap him. There was one, and only one, solution—take the best, leave the rest, and get out. His market outlet demanded prime quality logs for top quality lumber. There was no market for logs of inferior quality. There were no booming markets for salvage such as are now available in hardboard products, wood fuels, wood chemical products, plywood, and others. The only worth of a tree was in terms of boards. If it couldn't be converted into boards and construction timbers it was worth nothing. The best went to market. The rest was left to rot on the ground that had produced it.

On a blackberry picking mission one summer day, Mother and I rode a logging locomotive up toward Camp 7. Scars of the great fire were everywhere. The tremendous heat of the fire had turned live trees into blackened skeletons that marched silently and unwanted across the land. Felled trees and logging trash lay in immense heaps of charred waste. It was so still the soft sigh of the wind as it flowed around the tops and trunks of the snags sounded abnormally loud and reminded me of the sound of the Pacific Ocean surf. A hawk wheeled in watchful silence. A group of crows began chatting. They were beyond easy range of our eyes but their calls, raspy and urgent, crowded out the deathly stillness for a brief moment.

I didn't like the burn. It was as morbid and hateful and scary as visiting an abandoned area of hell. Mother said she didn't like it either. We walked on up the track but it was a long while before we were free of the burn and back in logged-over but unburned and more gentle land. Wild blackberry vines were everywhere and loaded with ripe, sun-sweetened berries. We picked, and talked as we picked.

Pointing north to the area of Big Creek and northeast to the rather isolated hump of rock and timber known as Nicolai Mountain, seven or eight miles distant, Mother commented upon the number of smoke pillars that marked the location of steam donkey engines and the fast-receding line of trees. "It's a long walk from here to green timber," she said. There was timber surrounding our vantage point, but the dozens of camps working in the area had slashed away so persistently that vast areas now lay in stubble and trash. Looking out over this churning empire of dogged machines and crumbling forest, one could see areas where groups of machines were working toward each other. It gave an onlooker the feeling of watching a pack of coyotes closing in on a victim. But here, high in the Coast Range of Oregon, the hunting packs were steam donkey engines and the victims were trees, tens of thousands of acres of trees.

On a clear day from the Camp 7 ridge, locomotives and donkey engines at work for the Big Creek Logging Company were often visible. If the wind was out of the east or northeast it sometimes carried the sound of Kerry Line locomotive whistles. The Kerry Line, mostly in neighboring Columbia County, was not only the biggest and busiest logging railroad line in our area, it was also the most bold, and energetic. To get his Columbia & Nehalem River Railroad from his log dump on the Columbia River into the rich timber belt of the Nehalem River Valley, owner A. S. Kerry punched a tunnel under a ridge of the Coast Range mountains. Kerry Line log trains often rolled day and night hauling a million board feet of logs through the tunnel between the dawn of one day and the dawn of the next. A dozen camps, operated by as many owners, fed their daily outputs to Kerry Line locomotives. A million board feet of logs, if sawed into lumber, is enough to build eighty or ninety average five-room houses.

South from the Camp 7 ridge loomed thirty-two-hundred-foot Saddle Mountain, a tremendous saddle-shaped mass of basalt belched up ages and ages ago from the interior of the earth during some catastrophic adjustment in the earth's surface. It towered over the rest of the thousand square miles of forest, waterways, mountains, and farmlands that make

up Clatsop County. Atop what would correspond to the horn
of a saddle was a tiny fire-lookout structure. Steel cables,
anchored to heavy pitons driven deep into the basalt, held
it in place against howling winds that sometimes swept across
the narrow, triangular top of the mountain.

Saddle Mountain was Mother's idea of primitive majesty.
"God placed it there to watch over Clatsop County and its
forests," she used to tell me. Looking out over the five or six
airline miles that separated it from us and our blackberry
patch, I wondered if it were really working for God. Plumes
of donkey engine smoke and steam rose skyward from ridge
slopes and canyons between it and us. And I knew that already donkey engines of the Saddle Mountain Logging Company were gnawing at a vast belt of timber almost at the
mountain's foot.

A great panic and sadness suddenly welled up within me.
I clutched at one of Mother's blackberry-picking hands. "I
don't want all the trees to be gone," I sobbed in boyish
agony.

There, in the sullen loneliness of a logged-off ridge top,
and surrounded by blackberry vines and with Saddle Mountain staring directly at us, Mother slipped both arms around
me and drew me close. A wetness that soaked through a
shoulder of my shirt told me that she was crying too.

"Trust in God and the mountain," she kept saying, between sobs, "I don't know how, but they'll see to it that
Oregon and Clatsop County will always have trees."

*Chapter 15*

# WELCOME HOME

It was a drizzly March evening in 1937. As I walked up the railroad track from the crossing to Big Sam's bunkhouse it pleased me to note that after fifteen years the ties and rock ballast underfoot had a familiar, welcome-home feel. The chuckling sounds of Klaskanine Creek were exactly as I remembered them. The smells of engine oil, timber, and wood smoke from heating stoves in homes and bunkhouses were rich, nostalgic, and like a tonic.

But there were changes. Shortly after Mother and I had moved to Seaside in 1922 so that I could continue school, the company had reorganized. The old familiar name Western Cooperage had been dropped. It was now Tidewater Timber Company. The spot where our house had sat on its log skids was empty and overgrown with alder trees and brush. The one-room school was gone. The Johnson family was gone. The old shop had been rebuilt into a larger, more modern structure. Bigger locomotives now handled the log trains. Some of them sat, resting, lined up end to end on a couple of shop sidings.

Big Sam was of an age when he could no longer work in the woods. His legs and wind, the vulnerable functionaries of a logger, years ago had rebelled at his driving will. In this respect a logger and a boxer have much in common. Legs and wind are the first to give out. Big Sam was moved to the shop crew. At first it was like harnessing an old fire horse to a buggy and ringing an alarm bell. He did everything on the run and fretted to be back in the woods.

"He's fidgeting hisself to death," Daddy Hoyt, white-bearded shop fireman and stationary-engine operator, said worriedly to Mother.

"Give him a little time," said Mother, "he'll quiet down."

After Mother and I moved to town Dad moved into an unoccupied bunkhouse near the shop. It was a two-bunk unit painted red. On school-vacation visits to the camp Mother would sometimes stay with friends and I'd stay with Dad in his bunkhouse. It was always exciting. Log trains coming in late at night or leaving in the predawn hours steamed by within spitting distance of the bunkhouse.

Now, in the half darkness of early evening, and with the cool, soft touch of a Coast Range drizzle in my hair, I was back. This time for good. Time and experience had convinced me. It was here, in this land of God and Big Sam, that I belonged.

Convincing Big Sam of that fact wasn't going to be easy. "Your father will be disturbed and hurt," Mother cautioned when I told her that three years of college were enough and that I was going to the camp and get a job.

As I stepped on the piece of plank that served as a walk between the railroad track and the bunkhouse doorstep I recalled Mother's words and knew she was right. I hoped he'd be mad when I told him. Anger is easier to deal with than a hurt. Big Sam must have read my mind. When I told him why I had come to the camp he was mad enough to uproot stumps.

"Of all the tomfool notions," he exploded, stomping around on the calk-splintered floor in his bare feet and long underwear. "With three years of college you want to be a logger." He sighed, shrugged, and blustered and marched around in his bare feet.

Keeping out of his way, I laid my suitcase on the empty bunk. Opening it, I removed a leather wallet, greeting card, and box of chocolates. "Before you get too mad," I said, "happy birthday. You were sixty-seven day before yesterday, in case you forgot." He stopped short, wordless and baffled. "The wallet and card are from Mother," I said, handing them over to him. "The candy's from me."

He studied the card for a moment, then handed it back. "Read it," he ordered, "I can't see in this light."

There was a message in Mother's handwriting. I read it out loud. It said: "Sam, dear, in addition to the wallet I'm sending you a twenty-five-year-old son who is just as stubborn and bullheaded as you must have been at that age. Watch over him."

Never in my whole life had I ever seen Big Sam look as though he might cry—even when they carried him in from the woods after a flying choker had driven its steel fist into his body and smashed a half-dozen ribs. But for a fleeting instant after I finished reading the card it looked as though he might. It was embarrassing for both of us. I turned out the light and in the sudden darkness stumbled toward my own bunk. I closed the suitcase and set it on the floor. I undressed, rolled back the canvas bedcover, and crawled between the logging camp sheets. I heard Big Sam doing the same. He brought blankets from home because he didn't like sheets. "Good night, Dad," I said. There was a sigh, but no answer.

The next morning I went up to the camp office and asked Ken Long for a job. He was the timekeeper and in charge of operations at the headquarters camp. Ken and his brother, Dave, were loyal friends and admirers of Big Sam's.

After talking with Ken I hunted up Big Sam in the shop. "I got a job," I said.

"In the woods?" was his first question. He was nervous and anxious.

I shook my head. "I wanted something suitable for a college man," I said, "and I got it. Working on the railroad section crew."

For the first time since I had arrived at camp the night before, Big Sam laughed. He laughed and laughed, and kept on laughing. I recognized it for what it was. Not a laugh intended to shame me for having to accept a menial job, lowest in pay and social rating of any job in a logging camp. It was a laugh mirroring relief and sweeping away of tensions. Big Sam had a deathly fear of me going to work on the big machines in the woods. The railroad section crew was as safe as a bleacher seat in a ball park. About the worst that could happen would be cramped muscles from shoveling and tamping ballast.

Helping lay new railroad spurs as well as tearing up and maintaining old ones brought me in direct contact with the various logging areas. Company holdings in the old Camp 7 and Camp 2 regions had long since been cleared of timber. The land was left a vast, silent waste of snags and stumps marching in melancholy dreariness across ridge and canyon for as far as the eye could reach. It left one with a feeling of shame and sadness. It reminded me of pictures I had seen of the tired white crosses in the Meuse-Argonne in France and Flanders Field in Belgium.

Instead of following Klaskanine Creek east up the canyon from the headquarters camp, the railroad now reached into mountainous timber belts to the southeast and on into the Nehalem River Valley beyond Jewell. The heavy sled-mounted logging engines were now crashing their way through thousands of acres of unbroken forest that when I was a boy hadn't yet felt the scuff of a logger's calk shoes. And the thunder-voiced machines no longer dragged logs flat on the ground. Highlead and skyline systems, slackline carriers and multiengined skidders, mounted on railroad cars and weighing a hundred tons, sent them thrashing and bounding across the land with one end clear of the ground like a fish being reeled in half out of the water.

This was the way they did it now. Fast, terrifyingly fast. Savage, brutal, and deadly. It got so there was almost as much logging equipment hanging over a man's head as there was on the ground.

"You stay on the section," Uncle Marsh once warned me.

"With these highleads and skylines a man ain't safe even under the ground." He had a point. The average main-line cable these days weighed between three and four pounds to the foot; a skyline almost seven and a half pounds. A heavy high-lead block dangling from the top of a spar tree one hundred and fifty or one hundred and seventy-five feet above your head would tip the scales at more than a ton. Lesser blocks for the maze of smaller cables along with guy lines to strengthen and steady the tree added more tons.

The section crew was safe enough but the pay was in pro-portion. In 1937 pick, shovel, and spike maul work on the section paid $5 a day. Lowest pay in the woods, whistle punk and choker setting, was $6.20. I knew, and I think Mother and Dad and Uncle Marsh knew too, that sooner or later I'd end up the same as Dad and Uncle Marsh, hus-tling rigging and fighting rain, mud, brush, dust, and sun at the far end of a main-line cable hooked to the reel-like drum of one of the big machines.

There were six months of section crew body hardening work before the opportunity came. It was six months of shoveling, swinging a spike maul, and wrestling railroad steel and railroad ties—six months that wiped off fraternity house beer fat, tempered arm and leg muscles grown soft from two winters and a summer of clerking in a grocery store.

Big Sam watched from the side lines and in his eyes there was a look of approval. "You look better," he admitted, somewhat grudgingly I thought. An entry in Mother's diary under Aug. 13, 1937, states that "Dad and Samuel home in evening. . . . Samuel looks brown and like a logger now."

Body toughening was only one of the rewards of hard physical work on the section crew. The main benefit was the opportunity to share a bunkhouse and hours of companion-ship with Big Sam. During my college years we had grown apart. In college the emphasis was on achievement. Day after day you were told that you were among God's chosen few.

A high school graduate's earning power was limited to a certain amount. A college graduate's had no end. You could go on and on and the money would keep flowing in. A man who stopped to admire a sunset was a fool. There was no pot of gold in a sunset. The only thing that mattered was the number of twenty-dollar bills in your wallet, your credit rating at the bank, the number of suits hanging in your closet.

Big Sam didn't shape up very well in the light of this new philosophy. His speaking English was atrocious. It was full of "I seen's" and "I ain'ts."

"There is no such word as 'ain't,' Mother was always reminding him.

"Then how come you just said it?" Dad would counter.

College made me terribly ashamed of Dad. I was embarrassed over his poor grammar and near inability to read or write, the old suit he wore which had been his wedding suit in 1911 when he married Mother. When I'd mention that he ought to have another suit he'd argue that since a man could only wear one suit at a time what was the sense in having two? It was all so ridiculous and absurd. Angry and frustrated, I'd go to Mother.

"There is more to life than two suits and money," she'd argue in Dad's defense, although during the early years of their marriage she had tried mightily to push him on toward greater things. Dad had inbred qualities—love, loyalty, integrity, and a dogged determination to do what was moral, honest, and right—that you don't buy, or borrow, she'd point out. Those are God-given, she'd say. She had a homemade saying: A man can make himself rich but only God can make him honest.

At the camp, after supper and before bedtime, Big Sam and I talked and got to know each other. I learned of his early life, his great love and admiration for Mother, his hopes and ambitions for me.

"This ain't no place to bury your life," he once told me, referring to the camp. He said he was a logger because he lacked education and couldn't do anything else. He was getting old and tired and felt he had been a failure.

Working at the camp, I explained, was the fulfillment of a boyhood dream. It was the only way in which I could satisfy this longing and urge to be like him. After years of virtually ignoring him, I wanted desperately for him to know how I really felt, how I loved, admired, and respected him. How Lew Mills, general manager of Tidewater Timber Company, had told me to be patient and work and he'd keep an eye open for something better, maybe in an industry related to the logging industry. Lew Mills took an interest in me not because I was Samuel Churchill who had majored in business administration at the University of Oregon. He had faith in me because I was Samuel Churchill, son of Big Sam. "You got a damn fine father," he told me gruffly, "and I hope you realize it." Lew was a graduate of Harvard. He had money, prestige, and influence, all the things that had seemed important to me in college. But he also had those God-given gifts of honesty, loyalty, kindness, and moral worth; and having them himself, he recognized them in Dad.

And he had one other attribute. He was big. Just as big and powerfully built as Uncle Marsh or Dad.

One early fall evening after supper I broke the news to Dad. "I'll be moving up to the summit camp tomorrow," I told him. I was leaving the section crew and going to work in the woods.

The old worried, uneasy look that was on his face when I first returned to the camp had come back. "Be careful," he said. "Keep your eyes on any moving line and watch where you step." It was simple advice but the kind that kept a man alive and off the injured list in a logging camp.

There wasn't much to moving. All my wordly goods could be packed in my suitcase, and with room to spare. When No. 53, a big Baldwin rod engine, powered into camp with a long string of empties, I tossed my suitcase onto the cab deck and climbed up after it. Jack Watson, the engineer, set the throttle out a couple of notches and the big, steam-bellied brute roared to life.

"Where you going?" he yelled over the blasting staccato of the firebox and stack.

"Joe Russoff's rig-up crew," I shouted back.

"A fellow your age ought to buy a piece of land and raise black walnuts," he yelled. "On a rig-up crew you end up dead or stove up." He was silent for a moment while apparently sizing me up, then added: "A college fellow could make a fortune raising black walnuts."

By now the big locomotive had entered a looping curve that carried it across Klaskanine Creek on a short trestle, the start of a winding three-mile climb to the company's Summit or Upper Camp, headquarters for the actual logging operations.

Seeming to hunch down for a firmer grip on the seventy-pound rail for the climb ahead, the powerful locomotive shattered the forest silence with violent eruptions from its stack that crashed against one's eardrums like claps of thunder. The interior of the firebox was a seething, rolling mass of screeching flame. Watson leaned down to shout in my ear. "Your dad helped build this piece of track." My throat was already raw from yelling. I knew the story, so I just nodded.

It had been in the fall of 1923 and the spring of 1924. The company had to get its railroad from the narrow canyon of Klaskanine Creek to the summit for high-altitude logging of fresh timber stands. The grade had to be held to a maximum of 3 per cent so heavy main-line engines such as No. 53 could be used. A number of surveys had ended in failure. Engineers said it couldn't be done. A thirty-two-year-old fellow by the name of Bob Shefler was finally brought in. He was a University of Oregon graduate and a trained rail-road location engineer. Company officials asked him what he needed. He said to start out with just an ax, a compass, and Big Sam.

There was four feet of snow at the summit and it didn't shallow up much at lower elevations. The two men took turns breaking survey trails through the snow and hacking out brush. The brutal work kept their bodies warm but their legs and feet were sometimes so numb with cold as to be insensitive to pain. Shefler sliced a shoe with his ax but was unaware of anything wrong until he noticed a trail of blood behind him. Both he and Big Sam were mystified by the blood until they stopped to check each other over and found blood welling out from the open slash half-hidden by frozen snow on Shefler's shoe. He sat shivering in the snow while Dad removed the shoe and sock. Dad bound the foot in a bandanna handkerchief. The cloth and cold stopped the blood flow. He replaced Shefler's sock, eased his foot back into the shoe, and they went back to work.

Shefler laid out a railroad grade that met company specifications. Lew Mills made him company superintendent. I last talked with him forty years later in late 1963, a few months before his death at the age of seventy-three. He was then living in Seaside and was Clatsop County's road engineer.

"He was all man, your father was," said Shefler, smiling in a reminiscent way. "My God, but he was strong."

Old 53 thundered her way through massive cuts and across towering trestles following the route grubbed through snow and brush by Bob Shefler and Big Sam fourteen years before. There was no snow on the ground on this fall day in 1937. And the cab of old 53 was hot as a fireroom in hell.

The summit camp sprawled over several acres of stump-littered ground on a sidehill shelf of land that reached back from the logging railroad yards where loaded cars from the logging areas were teamed up into long trains for the trip to the log dump at Olney. The summit camp was partially mobile. The bunkhouses, office, cookhouse, and dining rooms were built on railroad trucks so that they could be coupled into a train and moved by locomotives to new camp sites nearer the ever shifting logging areas.

I picked up my suitcase and swung down to the ground from the slow-moving engine. It felt its way along the numerous tracks, hemmed in by long strings of loaded log cars. In the distance smoke and steam from several donkey engines bolted skyward as cylinders pumped life into the big drums that reeled in the cables. Across a low-lying basin a big yarding engine was wrestling a log out of a canyon. Its whistle signals floated toward me sharp and clear. It was close enough that I could see the guyed spar tree quivering under the strain and hear the clanking grind of the heavy main-line drum gears and the snapping, whiplash sound of steel cables drawn rigid as a steel bar.

Death walked beside a man every minute of the day out there. It stalked a man with the precision and patience of a mountain lion belly-crouched and watching a deer. Big Sam had met it face to face a dozen times in his logging career. It pounced so unexpectedly. A flying limb coming at you like a bullet from nowhere. The thirty-pound steel fist of a choker driving at your head or belly with the whish of a rocket. Twenty tons of stubborn log suddenly cartwheeling in homicidal fury when caught in the main-line noose of a yarding donkey engine.

I knew that neither Big Sam nor Uncle Marsh, nor Mother, forty miles away in Seaside, would have a peaceful moment as long as I was out there, fair game for death and the big machines. But this was something that had to be done. It was a personal thing the same as when I removed my shoes and socks and raced across the bare log stringers of the abandoned trestle to prove to myself and Jake Johnson almost twenty years ago that I was a man, at least in courage. At this moment in 1937 I was satisfying a hunger that gnawed at me throughout high school and college. I was standing on a mountain ridge, looking out over a hundred square miles of uncut timber. I thought of Jack Watson and his advice to buy land and plant black walnut trees. Maybe Watson was right. Maybe there was a fortune in black walnuts. But I wasn't interested in making a fortune. What I had been long-ing for was exactly what I now had—calk shoes, snagged pants, a hard-weaved shirt and the occupation title of logger.

Joe Russoff, head of the rig-up crew, wasn't at all im-pressed with my decision to become a logger. Sizing up my hundred and sixty-five pounds of inexperience, he made a public announcement that rattled fir trees two hundred yards away. "Keeerist," he thundered. "I ask fer a man and they send me a Goddam ignorant college kid."

"That's Big Sam's boy," somebody told him.

"I don't give a Goddam whose boy he is," Russoff shouted. "I want a man. A logger man."

A crew member sidled up to me and whispered. "Don't mind Joe. The sonofabitch's pissed off at something but he'll get his ass off the hot stove after a bit and be all right."

Jim Joyce, the man who had taken over as camp super-intendent from Bob Shefler, wandered by near quitting time. "How's young Sam doing?" he asked Russoff. Loggers never resorted to the sneaky devices of the business world in checking up on an employee. They asked a blunt question and wanted a blunt answer. It didn't matter in the slightest that I was standing right there. I knew Joe Russoff would tell Jim Joyce exactly what he thought of me. And after what he had said earlier I was certain I knew what he'd say. When Joe Russoff answered I knew immediately why I always had and always would love, admire, and respect log-gers.

"Green as hell," said Russoff, almost glaring at me, "but he ain't afraid of work and that's more than I can say of these other bastards."

That night in camp Jim Joyce dropped by my bunkhouse. "Well, you got off on the right foot with Joe Russoff," he said.

"I don't see how you figure," I said.

"You gotta understand Joe," Joyce explained. "I can read him like a book. He likes you."

Working on a rig-up crew was fast-moving, tricky, and dangerous. But you learned something about almost every phase of logging from moving and positioning donkey engines to rigging up a two-hundred-foot spar tree and getting it in operational condition for logging.

Under Russoff's watchful eye and spirited cursings I learned the names and uses of the dozen or more types of blocks used to guide logging lines. I learned the difference between a bell clevis and a straight clevis, between a line socket and a butt chain swivel, the difference between a guy-line clevis and all the other clevises.

And I learned safety. "Watch that Goddam line," he was always screaming at me, "Stay on the uphill side of a moving log," or "Watch that sapling." It seemed to me it was constantly watch, watch, watch, watch.

"If I can keep you alive to payday we'll both be lucky," he moaned in exasperation one day.

"This is the one thing I wanted to do right, but everything I do, I do wrong," I said. "What's the matter with me?"

He was silent for a moment as though thinking over the question. "First off," he said, "you ain't doing everything wrong. Fact is you're shaping up into a pretty good logger. If I can keep you alive another two weeks you'll be a first-rate hand."

"You're lying right through your teeth and you know it," I said.

"No I ain't," he said seriously. "Your big trouble is that you jump at a thing before you think about what you're going to do when you get there. Don't be in such a Goddam all-fired hurry. And another thing, you're tryin' to be like your dad and your uncle and you ain't ever goin' to be. And that ain't no disgrace because there ain't many of these young pissers in the woods right now can keep up with your Uncle M____ and him bein' almost sixty."

: do I do about it?" I asked.

gotta decide that," he said, "but since you asked, I'd

get the hell out of the woods and buy a piece of land," he said.

"And what would you do with the land?" I asked.

"I'd plant it to black walnut trees and make a fortune," he said. For a moment I thought he was ribbing me. But he was dead serious.

"Joe," I said, "you've been talking to Jack Watson."

He looked a little sheepish. "I have," he admitted, "but Jack Watson's no fool. He sits in a locomotive cab warm and out of the weather while me and you slog around out here up to our ass in mud." That was logic there was no arguing with.

"If black walnut trees can make a guy so much money why isn't Jack Watson buying land and planting them?" I wanted to know.

"Me and Jack's too old," said Joe. "It takes twenty, thirty years maybe, for a black walnut tree to grow. It ain't the walnuts you want," he explained, "it's the wood. They use it for furniture or something."

"I don't know," I said. "Twenty years is a long time. I'd be forty-five."

"That's what I mean," he said. "You'd be younger than I am right now and gettin' richer'n Lew Mills."

A shouting blast from the whistle of the donkey engine ended the conversation. The half-hour lunch period was over. Joe jumped to his feet. "By God," he roared, glaring at me, "when that whistle blows that means off your ass and on your feet."

"Why's he ridin' you all the time?" our head rigger asked.

"According to Jim Joyce," I said, "it's because he likes me."

"If I was your age," he said, "you know what I'd do?"

"No," I said, "what would you do?"

"I'd buy me a piece of land," he said.

"And plant it to black walnut trees," I interrupted, finishing the sentence for him.

"That's right," he said, with a surprised look on his face. "You know about black walnuts?"

"Not one damn thing," I said, "excepting that if Jack Watson doesn't keep his mouth shut Tidewater Timber Company's going to end up a ghost camp."

He laughed. "That would be somethin' wouldn't it. Old Jack humpin' into the summit yards some morning with a long string of empties and not a piece of smoke, a loaded log car, or a human being in sight." He howled with delight at the mental picture of Jack Watson's fancied bafflement and consternation in such a situation.

"Something almost like that could happen," I pointed out. "They're moving a hell of a lot of logs out of here."

"I been thinkin' about that," he said, "and I guess maybe Joe and some of the others have, too. They figure maybe another four or five years logging and Tidewater will be through."

"Is that why you fellows are all interested in black walnut?" I asked.

He nodded. "Black walnut trees maybe ain't much," he said, "but they're better than nothin'."

## Chapter 16

## FAREWELL TO BIG SAM

One of my first off-work assignments after joining the Tidewater woods' crew and moving to the summit camp was persuading Big Sam to join the union. It wasn't a volunteer task. Lawrence Daggett, president of the union's local, ordered me to do it. Daggett was a high-climber, a fellow who spent his work days one hundred and fifty to two hundred feet above the ground topping trees and converting them with guy lines, line blocks, and other rigging into spar trees. His tools were a pair of climbing spurs strapped to his legs, a four-strand manila rope with a flexible wire core that held him to the tree and freed both hands, a specially made single-bit ax with a twenty-six-inch handle, and a short length of crosscut saw. The ax and saw dangled from lengths of rope anchored to a wide, reinforced leather belt similar to what some truck drivers and motorcyclists use. Suited up and ready to go to work in an eighteen-dollar pair of calk shoes, he was worth about a hundred bucks. In skill, experience, and daredevilry the figure would probably be closer to one hundred thousand.

"We want your dad in the union," said Daggett. Every working man in the two camps except the office crews, superintendent, and Big Sam were union members. Every logging camp on the Columbia River and elsewhere west of the Cascades was unionized. You joined the union or bought a farm and slopped pigs. If you wanted on a logging camp payroll you showed up with a union button or got one the first payday. The fellows weren't nasty about it but they let you know the rules and you took the ball from there.

Unions had their faults but they had to be credited with most of the major improvements in camp life. As a boy I remembered Dad and Uncle Marsh riding to and from the logging areas on open cars, exposed to the weather and with no safety devices. The unions made the operators replace the open cars with boxcar-like rail cars equipped with benches to sit on and a stove to warm up the interior. The union demanded and finally got for the men showers, sanitary outhouses, and sheets and mattresses on bunks instead of open straw as was furnished in the early days.

In Daggett's opinion, Big Sam was enjoying and benefiting from the union but not contributing. But he contributed in other ways. When the union took up a collection for Earl Pizer, a locomotive engineer with lung trouble, Big Sam gave more than any individual in camp. Daggett often confided in Big Sam. Jim Joyce, the superintendent, and Ken Long often let him in on company secrets. Each knew that whatever he told Big Sam never went any farther.

Big Sam was sixty-seven years of age and by law couldn't be forced to join a union. At least at that time and under the regulations in that area a worker sixty-five or over didn't have to join a union. I mentioned that to Daggett. He said that was correct but there was always the chance of some hothead hiring on and making trouble. Big Sam had weathered one such incident. A new head rigger decided he'd make Big Sam join or run him out of camp. Big Sam made most of the company's chokers and other rigging. But there isn't much that man can make that an eleven by thirteen or twelve by fourteen Humboldt yarder, such as Tidewater mostly used, can't tear to pieces if encouraged to do so.

This fellow encouraged the big machines to tear into Big Sam's rigging. But every time Big Sam's sockets and ferrules, babbitted at each end of a choker line, held; always, it was the cable itself that would finally break.

One night at a union meeting Big Sam's name again came up for discussion. Some of the fellows were getting a little impatient. This fellow reportedly stood up and gave Big Sam a verbal commendation, logger style. As it was passed on to me it went something like this: "When I got a piece of Sam Churchill's rigging around a log I know the sonofabitch is going to hold. It ain't going to bust up and smash me in the face or guts. I don't give a howl in hell whether he belongs to the union or not. I want him right where he is."

That sort of took care of Big Sam's union problem because every one of the two hundred or more men in camp knew this fellow had vowed to make Dad join the union or get out of camp.

But Daggett felt it would be even better if he did belong. I started down to the headquarters camp one evening after supper to talk it over with Big Sam. It was dark so I took the county road rather than risk a stumble on some of the high trestles on the railroad. The county road led me past the site of an old Douglas fir tree that Mother and I used to hike to summer and spring mornings when we lived at camp. It was a big, gruff old fellow about seven feet in diameter at stump height and more than two hundred feet tall. Dad estimated it to be close to six hundred years old. Using its age as six hundred years, Mother plotted out some key events in world history that it had lived through.

It must have been a fair-sized pole when the Black Death swept England in 1348. It was over one hundred and fifty years old and would have made a good trestle stringer when Columbus was sailing west across the Atlantic. It was full grown and showing its age by the time the first covered wagon train arrived in Oregon's Willamette Valley from Independence, Missouri, in 1843.

Mother named it "The Big Tree" and eventually the rest of the camp referred to it by that name and it became something of a landmark on the road to Jewell. Billy Deeds, driving his truck, might report seeing a cougar in the road a mile beyond the Big Tree from camp, or a bear just this side of the Big Tree.

During World War I a spruce camp was set up in a little canyon down from the county road just about opposite the Big Tree. The spruce loggers left it standing. Every time county road crews would come out to the area on a graveling or road widening project Mother would meet them, point out the Big Tree which was only ten or fifteen feet from the road's edge, and plead with them not to cut it down or harm it. There was still room for a couple of Model T Fords to pass, so she always got her way.

This particular evening, though, I didn't notice the old familiar bulk of the Big Tree. It had been several years since I had walked or driven along this portion of the county road but I knew from memory that the Big Tree should be in this immediate area. Retracing my steps and using a flashlight for a better look at the roadside, I inspected the immediate vicinity. The beam of the flashlight finally centered on a big stump. I knew without even going close that it was all that was left of the Big Tree. The stump was about twelve feet high and looked as though it had been weathering at least a couple of years. The notches that held the ends of the springboards on which the timber fallers had stood when they were chopping and sawing peered back at me along the flashlight beam like grinning Halloween pumpkin mouths.

It was a rather frightening shock to find the Big Tree gone. It was as though I was being reminded that the past was fast becoming a rotting shell and slipping beyond easy reach. It reminded me of the endless succession of changes that had passed over the old camp. Dozens of once familiar names and faces were gone. Dad and Mother had been living apart for fifteen years. The original move had been made so that I could continue grammar school. Now that my education was finished it was too late for Mother to return to the camp. Now she was completely alone except on weekends when Dad was home from the camp.

I realized with a shock that both Dad and the camp were getting old; that Uncle Marsh was no longer a young man; that the camp was old and tired and not far from retirement; that the last of the great primeval forest that so enthralled Mother when I was an infant was toppling under ax and saw and moving by the trainload from cutting areas to mills. It disturbed me to know that I was contributing to this destruction; to the end of Dad and Mother's personal era; to the end of a fascinating way of life—a remote but gay and carefree existence within a hand touch of God in Oregon's big timber. I was a full-fledged logger now. Joe Russoff had kept me alive and drilled home the lessons. I could take care of myself in any camp on the Columbia River. For the first time since the Camp 7 ridge incident with Mother I wanted to sit down and cry. Put the forest back on its rotting and weather-stained stumps. Push everything back twenty-five years in time and start over.

But there is nothing you can do about time. It flows past and beyond reach like a night wind in the trees. It brushes you in passing but leaves you behind.

I was no longer in a mood to talk to Big Sam about the union. I snapped the switch on the flashlight and sat on the ground beside the Big Tree's stump. With the light out the night blackness rushed in. I could hear the crunch of brush as deer stepped their way toward the creek in the gully behind me. A night owl sounded its hunting call. The tops of the trees gossiped with each other in the wind. I pictured the Big Tree as it was when I was a boy. Clothed in a cover of gnarled bark almost a foot thick. The limbs of its crown two hundred feet above the ground and some of them as thick as a man's body. A monarch that had fought off six centuries of wind, rain, and fire, only to fall chip by chip from the puny blows of an unknown timber faller's ax. Someday, I knew, Big Sam would fall, too.

I must have sat there by the stump for at least an hour. Anyway it was long enough that the moon finally started its night walk across the sky. I was chilled from sitting. I found myself wishing that Dad and Mother, the Big Tree, the old camp and everything else that was dear to me could be like the moon and live forever.

Sitting there for that hour or so, remembering, worrying, regretting, and wishing, left me more weary of muscle and mind than a full day's work. I got up, shook the chilled stiffness from my legs, and headed back up the road toward the summit camp.

Waiting on the plank platform in front of the office for the crew trains to load the next morning, Daggett spotted me. He wondered if I had had any luck convincing Big Sam to join the union.

"I didn't ask him," I said. "Anyway, why the hell bother him now?" I argued. "Look, Daggett, he's sixty-seven years old. He was here when they laid the first tie of the old Western Cooperage railroad in 1911, or maybe it was late 1910. Let him rest."

He gave me a playful poke in the ribs. "Don't worry about it," he said. "They ain't anyone here going to make it rough on Big Sam."

Each day it seemed the crew train had to travel a little farther to reach the logging area. It didn't really, but as the yarding engines dug deeper into the thinning band of forest we had to walk farther from the end of the rail line to get to the job. I had left the rig-up crew several months previous and was now setting chokers on a yarder. At the far end of a yarding donkey's main line you were within ear range of the crashing giants as ax and saw cut them down. You could almost feel the wall of green timber at your back retreating step by step, day by day.

And then there would be the day when it suddenly occurred to you that the line had moved back so far that you could no longer hear the swish and crash of falling trees hitting the ground. But pretty soon the big machines, dragging themselves forward foot by foot like a man stranded on the desert clawing ahead on his belly toward a distant water hole, would catch up and start feeding on new acres of felled timber.

And then one day in May 1941 the thing I had learned to dread happened. I was no longer working in the camps (I was now married and living in Yakima, Washington) but Mother sent me a newspaper clipping. The great machines had reached the crest of the last ridge. They sat there, steam up and fireboxes roaring. But there was no more timber. Lawrence Daggett rigged the last spar tree and when the last log had been dragged in he helped unrig it and herd the jobless machines toward railroad loading sites for their last ride on Tidewater Timber Company rails.

I wondered if Jack Watson, or Joe Russoff, or that head rigger would now plant their black walnut trees. I wondered what Uncle Marsh would do with his calked shoes. I wondered how long it would take the alder, elderberry, salmonberry, fern, moss and other natural vegetation to crowd in and take back the land and obliterate the many things of the camp that was my birthplace and my home town.

After thirty years of living it didn't seem possible that it would all now in a short time be dead—that scrap handlers would go to work on the donkey engines and steel rail with cutting torches and do to them exactly as they had done to the forest. I hoped that some of the innocent locomotives that had been a part of my life for so long would escape a flaming death from the searing blue heat of a torch and maybe find jobs on some of the few remaining logging railroad lines.

The machine shop and parts of the railroad were to continue in operation for another year while a logging firm or two that used the Tidewater rail line finished up their timber. Big Sam, now seventy-one years of age, had another year's work ahead of him. I worried about him. He wasn't the type who could retire gracefully and live at peace with the world on Social Security. Big Sam had to be active. He wouldn't live a year without a steady job.

It was agony to me knowing that one day Big Sam would come home from the camp for the last time, that fifty years of life in the big timber would just suddenly end. I wondered how a company would handle such a situation. You walk up to a man who has given you thirty years of his life. A man who was there when the first tree was felled and the land all around was virgin and waiting. And who was still there after the last tree had been cut and the last log was bobbing gently in the waters of Youngs River, waiting for its place in the last raft to float from the dumping grounds at Olney.

What do you say when you walk up to a man like that on his last day? Do you say, "Here's your check, Sam. Thanks for your thirty years of loyalty and good work. Don't forget, you can sleep in in the morning."

Suddenly, I wanted to be with Big Sam. I wanted to talk with him, be with him. Mother I didn't worry about. She could adjust. Big Sam was different. Ax and saw and the big machines had ended, for him, a way of life. It was as though the waters of the Columbia River had suddenly siphoned away from under old Captain Hosford, leaving him high and dry when he and the *Georgiana* still had hope and were going strong.

Decoration Day, a holiday where I worked and also for Dad in the shop, came on a Friday in 1941. I took a plane to Portland and a bus from Portland to Seaside. It seemed rather absurd to take money from the small amount my wife and I had laid aside in the savings account at the bank for arrival of a possible third generation Big Sam sometime in August. But there was this driving urge to be with Big Sam. I had cancelled my plane reservation once, but my wife had insisted I reinstate it and go see Mother and Dad.

I arrived home in Seaside at nine-thirty on a Thursday evening. I know the exact hour because Mother kept track of such things in her diaries. Dad had already arrived home from camp for the holiday. We talked late and were up again early Friday morning. I helped Dad pile a load of wood for a neighbor. We chopped some wood for Mother, mowed and raked the lawn, walked on the beach and talked.

Dad wanted to know when he was going to be a grand-father. Near the end of August, I told him. He smiled in anticipation. I asked him about the old camp. He shrugged. The talk, he said, was that the railroad and shop would keep going another year. It was sad, he admitted, to see flatcars of steel rail go clattering through camp on their way to some scrap pile and to see the once-proud steam donkey engines slashed to pieces by cutting torches.

But it was sadder still, he said, to know that the timber was gone. He shook his head in what was almost a motion of disbelief. In his mind was the picture of the endless sweep of green timber he and Uncle Marsh had looked out over from that crest of hill in Portland in 1902. And there were the words of Uncle Marsh that had seemed so logical and true on that day in 1902: "They'll be logging here a thousand years from now. You mark what I say, Sam. A thousand years from now."

Dad and Mother walked with me to the bus depot. It was a little before 2:20 P.M., Sunday, June 1. The passengers were starting to enter the bus. I leaned over and kissed Mother. I held out my hand and Dad took it. The touch of his hand was reassuring. The fingers, at seventy-one years of age, were still heavy and hard as steel. "Don't worry," I said.

"What's there to worry about?" he said.

I turned and followed the line of passengers into the bus. I didn't know it then, but I had just shaken hands and said good-by to Big Sam for the last time. On the morning of July 30, 1941, he just dropped off to sleep on the job with the sounds of the air hammers, forge work, and diesel power plant in his ears. It was a Wednesday. In her diary that morning Mother had written "Wednesday. A nice day."

We put Big Sam to rest where we thought he'd like to

be—under a tree in Astoria's Ocean View Cemetery between the surf sounds of the Pacific and the Coast Range where he and Mother had come as newlyweds and the big machines once roamed.

It was a cloudy day with a heavy mist rolling in from the sea. It was the kind of day Dad and the Coast Range loved. Throughout the service I couldn't help but think how God had seemingly planned this whole thing.

The old camp, Big Sam, and Oregon's big timber had spent most of a lifetime together. Now, they were being buried, within months of each other.

## Chapter 17

## THE NEW BREED

On a recent visit to the old headquarters camp site I was surprised to find a new generation of loggers at work there. They had turned the old railroad grade that went by Rex Gaynor's house, and where Fen Johnson and I found the cougar tracks in the snow, into a graveled truck road. Apparently they were logging the belt of timber that stood between us and the Camp 7 fire on that day and night of terror in 1918. In the days of the Western Cooperage it wasn't good enough.

Remains of the old machine shop had been pushed aside and farther into the brush. Logs were now stacked about where Mr. Casey's locomotive had sat on the day when I climbed up into its cab and told Mr. Casey I was scared and maybe something real terrible was going to happen, maybe a fire.

I drove on up the old Western Cooperage railroad grade, now a graveled fire patrol and access road. I reached the area where I thought Camp 7 had been. It was difficult to see out across the land now. A new generation of trees, fifteen and twenty feet tall crowded the slopes and pushed eagerly and determinedly to the very edges of the road. There were great gaps in the once forested area but there were also thousands and thousands of acres of lush, vigorous new growth. I thought of the day in this same vicinity when I broke into sobs and told Mother I didn't want all the trees to be gone. And I remembered how she had cried with me and assured me that God and old Saddle Mountain, peering

out at me from under a cloud cover even as it had on that
day so long ago, would see to it that Oregon and Clatsop
County would never be without trees.

And I could remember Uncle Marsh slapping his thighs
and laughing like a maniac when Mother suggested that someday loggers might plant trees. And now that day had come
to pass. God, Saddle Mountain, and man were working together. Where Mother and I had looked out over hundreds
of square miles of cropped and gutted land I was now looking
out over hundreds of square miles of young, watched-over
forests.

I wished Mother and Dad could be standing beside me,
looking. Dad would have been pleased but he wouldn't have
said much. I knew what Mother would have done. She
would have done what I was doing at the moment, crying.
I could feel the streams of tears bunching up along my jaw
line. I brushed them away with a handkerchief. It seemed
rather silly for a grown man to be standing alone on a memory ridge and bawling. But I wasn't ashamed.

I drove back down the road to the old camp. I rummaged
around in the brush until I found the skeleton remains of an
old outhouse in the area where I thought our house might
have sat. I couldn't say for a certainty whether it was ours
or not. Forty-seven years is a long time for even the memory
of an outhouse to last. I walked over to where the old
county road bridge used to cross Klaskanine Creek. A sturdy
concrete structure had taken its place. The builders hadn't
provided any flat surfaces along the top of the railings on
which sons of this new generation of loggers could have foot
races.

Standing at the camp side of the bridge, I looked up the
creek to where the Johnsons' house had stood. It was just
brush and alder but for a fraction of a second I thought I
saw the old shake house setting there and old Mrs. Johnson,
in slippers and smoking her pipe, sweeping off the log step.

I walked on up the road the mile to the stump of the

Big Tree. I wondered how close Dad had come those many years ago to estimating its correct age when he guessed it at six hundred years. I climbed to its table-like top and brushed away a layer of moss, needles, and other growth to expose a narrow strip from the outer rim to the center so I could count the growth rings. Each season a tree adds a growth ring to its outside skin, next to the bark. By counting the rings you can tell how old it is. Some of the rings were difficult to identify but I counted more than five hundred and eighty and that would have been the age of the old giant when it was cut down. It pleased me to know that Big Sam had come so close.

The old stump was doing its best to perpetuate forest life. A good-sized hemlock had taken root in part of its rotten wood. On its top a huckleberry bush and several hemlock seedlings were reaching for life.

I sat on the ground at its base just as I had done on that evening back in 1937 when I had started out to give Big Sam a sales pitch on why he should join the union.

In front of me, across the road and several hundred yards up the slope and hidden by alder and new forest growth, was the old railroad grade that Bob Shefler and Big Sam had surveyed through brush and snow almost forty years ago to the year. The rails were gone and the earth hadn't felt the weight of a locomotive or loaded log car for twenty years, but the trail was there, winding and climbing its lonely way toward a camp and a way of life that no longer existed.

Its only purpose now was to serve as a link between me and the past. Resting my head against a thigh of the Big Stump which had once been the Big Tree, I closed my eyes and listened. There was old No. 53 blasting its way toward the summit with Jack Watson at the throttle and a long string of empties and an oil tank car or two trailing along. I could hear her clattering over the overhead trestle that carried the railroad over the highway. And there was her full-throated whistle as she whistled for the crossing farther up.

And another whistle as she approached the yards where I had stepped from her cab with suitcase in hand and joy in my heart at finally becoming a logger.

And there was old Joe Russoff giving me hell and at the same time worrying about me. And Uncle Marsh looking at me in complete disgust when I told him I was on Joe's rig-up crew and going to be a logger.

And there were Ken and Dave Long at the headquarters camp office, always being helpful and kind and keeping an eye on Big Sam for Mother and me.

Ken is still living and resides in Portland, Oregon. But most of the old Western Cooperage camp faces and a big share of those from my Tidewater days are gone. The land and its ways have changed. Even the county road is no longer the same. It is now State Highway 202 and surfaced from Astoria, past the old camp, over the summit, and beyond Jewell into what used to be Kerry Line country, and Clark & Wilson country, and Oregon-American Lumber Company country.

The days of isolation that Mother knew are no longer. Automobiles and trucks whizz across the land where the big trees and the loggers once roamed. Astoria is only a half-hour's drive away. Aircraft fly overhead and the whine of their jet engines seems foreign and out of place in this land that had thrived in the era of steam.

Even the new generation of loggers working the patch of timber near the old headquarters camp has a different look. They wear hard hats for safety, live in town and drive out to the job each day. They go to football games in Astoria at night, belong to civic and service clubs, study up on politics, belong to the Parent-Teacher Association, have kids who hope to become doctors and lawyers, or physicists, or even foresters.

Nowadays they grow and harvest trees the same as farmers with field crops. The big companies plan their operations not days or months or years ahead, but centuries ahead.

The way they do it now makes Uncle Marsh something of

a seer because his prediction to Dad in 1902 that they would be logging in Oregon a thousand years from then is no exaggeration. It hasn't come about in the manner that Uncle Marsh expected. But what does it matter? What he said would happen is happening. The trees are coming back and this time they are back to stay.

I climbed to my feet and looked skyward from the stump of the Big Tree that was no longer there. Its place in the sky was being filled by the limbs and trunks of younger, more vigorous forest. I had a feeling that the old stump recognized me and remembered those earlier days when it had supported a giant and Mother and I had walked the mile from camp to admire and pay it homage each spring and summer morning.

The tree had served its time and a new generation of trees were taking over.

It was the same with our family. Dad was gone, Mother was gone, and Uncle Marsh was gone. The young hemlock pushing from the wood of the old stump was symbolic of the new breed. Life never really dies. It disappears in one form but reappears in another. Mother and Dad and Uncle Marsh, I was certain, were somewhere nearby, the same as the stump of the Big Tree. They had left me behind to carry on, even as the old stump was giving anchorage, food, and encouragement to the young hemlock.

Years ago I had left the woods and now there was no real desire to go back. I loved coming here; at intervals throughout the year tremendous urges seized me and forced me to return. Sometimes it might be for only a few hours of looking and remembering. It reminds me of the longing that sends the geese heading south for the winter, and north for the summer.

The old Western Cooperage camp will be a part of my life for as long as I live. Big Sam's footprints are cast in the wild, rugged breast of this magnificent land. Once I had hopes of leaving the imprints of MY calk shoes alongside his. But that was a boyhood dream with little chance of fulfillment. God and Saddle Mountain long ago decreed that this land would never really be mine. It is and will always be a monument to one man—my dad, Big Sam.

And as Lawrence Daggett once said:

"There will never be another BIG SAM."